HARD AGROUND

Library and Archives Canada Cataloguing in Publication
Title: Hard aground : untold stories from the Pollux and Truxtun disaster / Bett Fitzpatrick.
Names: Fitzpatrick, Bett, author.
Identifiers: Canadiana 20220414246 | ISBN 9781989417591 (softcover)
Subjects: LCSH: Truxtun (Ship) | LCSH: Pollux (Ship) | LCSH: Wilkes (Ship) | LCSH: Shipwrecks—Newfoundland and Labrador. | LCSH: World War, 1939-1945—Naval operations, American. | LCSH: St. Lawrence (N.L.)—History.
Classification: LCC VK1255.T7 F58 2022 | DDC 971.8/03—dc23

Published by Boulder Books
Portugal Cove-St. Philip's, Newfoundland and Labrador
www.boulderbooks.ca

Design and layout: Tanya Montini
Editors: Mallory Burnside-Holmes, Stephanie Porter
Copy editor: Iona Bulgin
Cover photo by Ena Farrell Edwards, courtesy of Rick Edwards.

Printed in Canada

We acknowledge the financial support of the Government of Newfoundland and Labrador through the Department of Tourism, Culture, Arts and Recreation.

Funded by the Government of Canada   Financé par le gouvernement du Canada   Canada

Untold stories from the *Pollux* and *Truxtun* disaster

HARD AGROUND

Bett Fitzpatrick

BOULDER
BOOKS

*To the memory of Ena Farrell Edwards, a main character
in my story and in the everyday life
and history of St. Lawrence.*

*With gratitude to the St. Lawrence Historical Advisory Committee,
the Lawn Trails of Heroes Committee, and Jimmy Rogers (Webbers)
for their dedication to keeping alive the events of February 18, 1942,
when three American warships ran aground on our shores,
their crews rescued by our people.*

PLACENTIA BAY AND THE BURIN PENINSULA

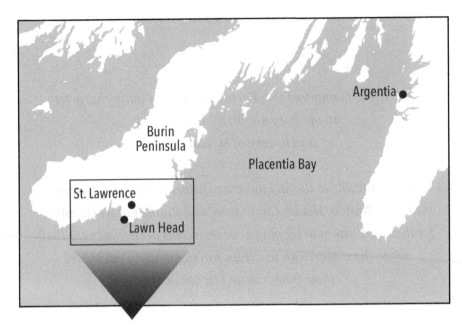

INSET: GROUNDING LOCATIONS OF THE *WILKES*, *POLLUX*, AND *TRUXTUN*

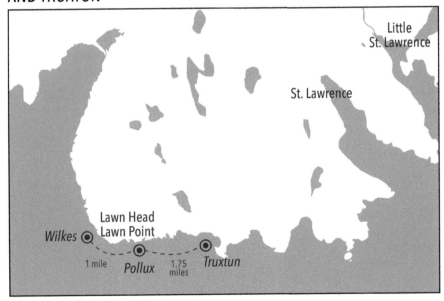

In 1942, the island of Newfoundland, off Canada's east coast, was a colony of Great Britain. That country was embroiled in World War II. As the most easterly point in North America, Newfoundland was vital to the defence of Canada and the United States. US president Franklin D. Roosevelt, an ally of Britain, provided the British Navy with 50 aging destroyers in return for US access to bases along the coast of Newfoundland. The US officially entered World War II in December 1941, following the Japanese attack on Pearl Harbor.

German submarines crossed the Atlantic Ocean to attack American and Canadian merchant ships carrying supplies and troops bound for Europe destined for the war effort. Naval escorts for North American vessels were essential.

At 0800 hours, February 16, 1942, a convoy of three US Navy warships steamed out of Casco Bay Naval Base, Portland, Maine, bound for Argentia Naval Station, Placentia Bay, Newfoundland. The USS *Pollux*, a cargo ship converted to the war effort, was under escort. Flanking her starboard and port were the USS *Wilkes*, Flagship Destroyer Division 26, and the USS *Truxtun*, a four-stack destroyer.

CHAPTER 1
USS TRUXTUN

"Red ass."

Ensign Frederick Ardel Loughridge USNR bristled at the term.

It was Navy lingo for new officer graduates. Adding to the insult, he was a reservist, unlike the men of the regular Navy, who had come up through the ranks earning their titles. Reservists were generally thought of as below grade, to be tolerated, not to be listened to.[1]

Loughridge had graduated from Boston's Northeastern University and gone through officer training before being called to active duty by the Bureau of Navigation. As a junior officer, he was mentored by both superior officers and crew as he went about his duties and earned warfare qualifications. It amounted to on-the-job-training. He planned to make the most of his access to the chart room and his superiors. He hovered as Lieutenant Commander Ralph Hickox and Lieutenant Arthur Newman, the navigator, discussed their predicament. Newman's tone was terse. "I haven't been able to grab a navigational fix since we rounded Cape Sable, Nova Scotia, shortly after 0600 hours."[2] He drew in a breath.

Hickox, leaning over the charts, straightened up. "What about a star fix?"

Newman shook his head. "Negative. Nothing at all." He flicked his pencil onto the charts.

Loughridge looked on. He was not surprised. A star fix in this rotten weather? Not likely. And probably not unusual on the North Atlantic—

---

1   Cassie Brown, *Standing into Danger* (Toronto: Doubleday, 1979), 19.
2   Brown, *Standing into Danger*, 22.

in winter or summer. Newman, however, was antsy about sailing so far without pinning down an accurate position. Hickox, too, wore a sober expression. Approaching land and being unsure of their ship's location was not a position either of them wanted to be in.

The *Truxtun* was travelling in convoy from Portland, Maine, to Base Roger, Argentia, Newfoundland. Though her regular assignment was the North Atlantic, where she ranged north and south from Iceland to the Caribbean, her sizable fuel capacity qualified her for escort duty. On this run, the *Truxtun* was tied to the orders of the *Wilkes*. The *Wilkes* was one of the Navy's most modern and technically advanced destroyers. The *Truxtun*'s position was patrolling 2,000 to 3,000 yards on the port bow of the *Pollux*—roughly the same distance as the *Wilkes* from her starboard bow. Often assigned flagship duties when operating in convoy,[3] the *Wilkes* was responsible for all three ships. She set their course and speed. The *Pollux*, the formation guide, was tasked with maintaining that position. But she was not doing a good job. The *Wilkes* radar indicated that the *Pollux* wandered.

The *Pollux* had been converted for the war effort into a general stores ship serving with the Atlantic Fleet on regular provisioning cruises.[4] Several tales in circulation accounted for why the *Pollux* rated an escort. One was that she was shipping a secret cargo: radar, to be installed on destroyers operating out of Argentia. Another touted the *Pollux* as a floating national bank. Whatever the facts, all aboard the *Truxtun* recognized that monitoring the *Pollux*'s movements was top priority, though no easy feat.

The convoy left Casco Bay on February 16. To avoid the threat of German submarines, the vessels followed Zigzag Plan 26,[5] which could be likened to navigating a series of switchbacks, but on high seas: leave

---

3   George Stewart, "Naval Disaster in Newfoundland," October 28, 2015, Naval Historical Foundation, http://www.navyhistory. org/2015/naval-disaster-in-newfoundland.

4   Stewart, "Naval Disaster in Newfoundland."

5   Brown, *Standing into Danger*, 4.

base course, travel 1.5 miles left, execute a 40-degree change every three minutes, travel five minutes back on base course, followed by the same to the right. Then repeat in reverse. Although Plan 26 helped to avoid trailing U-boats, it also succeeded in sending the crew hurtling left and right for the buckets. It was enough to turn a cast-iron stomach.

Without landmarks or star sights, all three ships in the convoy navigated by dead reckoning: calculating a new position based on a previous fix, such as a radio station. This was then corroborated with astronomical observations. Loughridge thought the chances of the *Truxtun*'s navigator grabbing a star fix in this weather were slim. He was also aware that the ship, a fossilized four-stack destroyer (often referred to as a *four piper*), unlike the *Pollux* and the *Wilkes*, carried no fathometer to measure ocean depth soundings and help pin her position.[6] The *Wilkes*, as the flagship, had also been able to snag radar.

Still, Loughridge trusted that the *Truxtun*, crewed by 156 sailors, was in good hands with Hickox and Newman, both experienced officers. However, they had no control over the deteriorating weather conditions or the roaming *Pollux*. Regardless of the weather, or the antics of the *Pollux*, the convoy was under orders to arrive at Argentia at precisely 1200 hours on February 18. The winds had strengthened, blowing heavy snow across the *Pollux*'s bow. Loughridge braced himself.

His ship and her crew were in for a rough run.

Edward Louis Bergeron, Seaman 2nd Class USN, of Cambridge, Massachusetts,[7] had just survived eight strenuous weeks of boot camp at the newly renovated Naval Training Station, Newport, Rhode

---

6   Brown, *Standing into Danger*, 22..
7   Wayde Rowsell, *Waves of Courage: A WWII True Story of Valour, Compassion, & Sacrifice* (Truro Heights, NS: Dion Rowsell, 2019), 153.

Island.[8] He had done weapons training and daily physical conditioning exercises and learned basic grooming, Navy chain of command, knots and splices, flag signals, rifle-over-your-head drills, basic watch standing, shipboard damage control and how to scrub clothes and pull oars in a boat, and more—on next to no sleep.[9]

Bergeron had taken it all in stride. Though slight of build compared to some of his mates, he was proud of his new muscle. He felt strong and was eager to begin his new assignment aboard the *Truxtun*. Once aboard ship, Boatswain's Mate 1st Class Harry (Boats) Egner addressed the 15 new recruits assembled midship (who had no sea training at all) and told them to forget everything they'd learned ashore. "We're sailing into war," he warned. "It's no cushy training barracks." Egner was right. None of his weeks of basic training, not week four of watch standing, nor week five's shipboard damage control practices, had prepared him for tonight.

Bergeron had pulled the 0000-to-0400-hour watch. Just his luck. He rubbed his eyes and attempted to sit up. He was still getting used to the duty system of four hours on duty and four hours off and had barely slept. The bucking and rolling of the ship hadn't helped. The weather, a mess of snow and sleet stirred to a frenzy by the gale, had grown messier through the evening—and probably had worsened even more while he slept. He groaned at the thought and hoped that the wandering *Pollux* wouldn't ram them on his watch. The tub was never where she should be, not even yesterday in passable weather. Egner had warned the new recruits as they chowed down in the mess that she'd sometimes show up much too close for comfort. In any case, the *Pollux* certainly wouldn't be on track on a savage night like this. Bergeron and the other lookouts would have to keep a sharp watch.

---

8   No information could be found as to which of the four training stations on the east coast Bergeron attended. Newport seems to be the most likely. All were undergoing additions and renovations to accommodate increasing numbers of recruits.

9   "Recruit Training Command, Great Lakes, Illinois," http://en.wikipedia.org/wiki/Recruit_Training_Command,_Great_Lakes,_Illinois.

Before he could ease himself from his bunk, he was thrown out and tumbled to the deck. He swore, louder than he meant to. Rubbed his elbow. He should have listened to the old-timers in the mess earlier that evening and tied himself in.

Shoulder to the bulkhead, feet gripping the deck, he pulled on his Navy blues.

▼▲▼

Eighteen-year-old Lanier W. Phillips, Mess Attendant 3rd Class USN, was a Black man in a white man's Navy. Assigned to the messman branch—a racially segregated part of the US Navy, responsible for feeding and serving officers—Phillips was restricted to serving as a mess attendant,[10] except in the event of an attack, when he would report to a designated battle station. For him, that was the ship's bow; using insulated gloves, his job would be to grab hot shell casings and heave them over the side.[11]

Phillips and the three other Black seamen—William (Billy) Gene Turner, Mess Attendant 2nd Class; Earl Frederick Houston, Mess Attendant 2nd Class; Henry Garret Langston, Officer's Steward 3rd Class—and Filipino Tomas Dayo, Officer's Cook 1st Class, were assigned the drudge work: preparing and serving meals and hot and cold drinks, washing glassware, collecting laundry and garbage, stocking the heads and the galley, polishing silverware and officers' shoes, serving and cleaning in all capacities—and being all-round waiters to the officers.[12] When the weather was messy, like tonight, cleaning took most of Phillips's time—especially with green recruits on board with their tetchy stomachs. They kept him hopping, wiping up

---

10   The messman branch was the only branch in which Blacks could enlist until recruiting for general service was opened to them on June 1, 1942.

11   Rowsell, *Waves of Courage*, 205.

12   Michael E. Ruane, "Shipwreck Survivor Recalls How Town Altered His Idea of Race," *The Washington Post*, September 16, 2010, https://www.washingtonpost.com/wp-dyn/content/article/2010/09/15/AR2010091507189.html.

their misses and near-misses in the heads, spatterings on the railings, and around the buckets secured in nooks on deck and below. It was a job for three men.

Phillips was glad when evening came. Because conditions were too rough for a hot meal, officers and crew had to settle for cold sandwiches, which always caused considerable grumbling among the enlisted men, at least, and put a damper on their spirits. This miserable night the mood was mopey. Most stayed away altogether; not like evenings when the room was hoppin', lively with new recruits jabbering away, or eyes glued on the old-timers frightening the skivvies off the younger recruits with tales of wicked storms and near misses with icebergs.

Whenever he could, Phillips would gear down his plate-scraping and table-wiping and perk his ears.[13] The talk was often of German U-boats operating in the Cape Sable–Cape Race area—the stretch they were sailing now. Torpedo Alley, the men called it. The green recruits at the table gnawed on their sandwiches. The prospect of playing cat and mouse with the Germans at night, in these seas, was enough to choke a fellow's appetite. One sailor recalled that just over a week ago a German U-boat had sunk a British steamer off Cape Sable. At that, the remaining few finished their drinks and did not linger. In four hours, they'd be back on duty no matter how scared, or sick, they were.

After they'd gone, Houston wiped the tables while Phillips grabbed a bite in the mess attendants' pantry, segregated from the enlisted crew and so cramped that there was only room to stand. Later, as he wiped and stacked dishes, Phillips turned all the talk over in his mind. He had grown up in the South. The son of sharecroppers, great-grandson of slaves. He recalled his great-grandmother's words: "Never look a white man in the eye.... If you do, you'll get a whipping,

---

13   Sharon Adams, "Cold Comfort," *Legion Magazine*, February 1, 2017, https://legionmagazine.com/features//coldcomfort. Lanier Phillips taped interview.

or maybe lynched." For all his 18 years, Phillips had kept his head down, avoiding the Klan.[14]

As a child, Phillips had been sent to live with his aunt in Chattanooga, Tennessee, after the Klan had burnt down the elementary school built by his community in Lithonia, Georgia. In Chattanooga, he became best friends with James Henderson Foster. On October 27, 1941, having completed high school, both he and Foster enlisted in the US Navy—to get away from the South. They went through boot camp together and asked for assignments aboard the *Truxtun*. Phillips was assigned to the *Truxtun*, but Foster, Mess Attendant 3rd Class, went to the *Pollux*.[15]

The two friends had taken their chances joining the Navy. They'd have to take their chances with Torpedo Alley too.

▼▲▼

Loughridge stayed on the bridge after his 1200-to-1600-hour shift had ended.

In these deteriorating conditions an extra body topside would be appreciated, he felt. Winds had intensified throughout the day and a nasty blizzard brewed, conjuring combinations of snow, sleet, and hail and slinging it full force in the *Truxtun*'s path. Visibility was reduced to near zero, hampering attempts to nail down effective RDF (radio direction finder) bearings. No training cruise had prepared Loughridge for weather and seas like this—though he was convinced that the brass would have relished manufacturing this level of misery. A heavy North Atlantic gale pushing a full-blown blizzard in front of it was more experience under his belt.

The officers and crew remained watchful for U-boats and drifting icebergs as they laboured to maintain position on the *Pollux*. Darkness

---

14   Ruane, "Shipwreck Survivor Recalls."
15   Rowsell, *Waves of Courage*, 203-204.

came early, due to blizzard conditions, and with it they lost track of the other two ships. The noisy ocean prevented the sonar from picking up the sound of the *Pollux*'s propellers. Without a fathometer, they couldn't take ocean depth soundings, and they were travelling too fast in deep water to use the hand lead. Having lost contact, Hickox passed the order to stop zigzagging.[16]

Loughridge was relieved. Zigzagging, without being able to fix position on the *Pollux*, was unsettling. Unlike the *Pollux*'s captain, at least Hickox had leeway to make the call. He and Newman concurred that reverting to base course and reducing speed to 12 knots should allow for the zigzag of the convoy while maintaining their position on her port bow.

Loughridge supposed that by holding base course and estimating the *Pollux*'s speed and course, they could stay in position—under clear sailing, maybe. But tonight? In this gale and the weather worsening by the hour? Not likely, in his judgment. He left the chart room to grab a coffee and sandwich in the wardroom, but was back on the bridge at 1945 hours for his next shift.

At 2000 hours, the convoy left Nova Scotia waters and steamed for the centre of the mouth of Placentia Bay, located on the southeast coast of Newfoundland and bordered by the Avalon Peninsula to the east and the Burin Peninsula to the west. They were 155 miles from their destination: Base Argentia, on the east side of the bay, and about 70 miles to the north of open water.[17]

Placentia Bay was large and known for unpredictable currents that shifted with the prevailing winds. At 2300 hours, Hickox, leaning over the chart, peered up at Loughridge. "Have the sound operator attempt to pick up the *Pollux*."

Loughridge waited. The sound gear had a listening and echo-

---

16   Brown, *Standing into Danger*, 22.
17   Stewart, "Naval Disaster in Newfoundland."

ranging effect. He reported back to Hickox that the operator had briefly picked up the sound of the *Pollux*'s propellers on their starboard quarter. Loughridge ventured to ask, nerves making his voice louder than he intended, "So it appears we're still in position?"

Hickox, eyes glued to the chart table, grunted.

In the radio shack, the operator tried repeatedly to fix RDF bearings on Cape Race, Newfoundland, and Gallantry Head, St. Pierre Island. From Cape Race came a steady stream of static; from Gallantry Head, no sound of a beacon operating.[18]

At 2345 hours, Ensign William Maddocks entered the chart room. Loughridge stood by, all ears, as Ensign James Seamans, the previous officer of the deck (OOD), briefed Maddocks at the chart table. Running a pencil across the chart, he said, "Here's our track, running up the middle of Placentia Bay."

Maddocks nodded. "So, by 0400 hours we expect to be approximately 25 miles southeast of Ferryland Head?"

Loughridge recalled Ferryland Head from his study of the charts. "That's that last headland on the west side of the entrance to Placentia Bay."

The officers nodded.

Seamans, in his succinct manner, gave a rundown of their situation: No fathometer aboard meant no soundings, RDF bearings were diminishing as they steamed north, and they were moving too fast to use the hand line.

Uppermost in Loughridge's mind was St. Pierre Bank, one of several shelves that formed the Grand Banks, a fishing ground southeast of the island of Newfoundland. St. Pierre Bank was used by mariners sailing Placentia Bay to fix ocean depth, and thereby their position, when factoring how close they were to land. In fact, it was their only chance to do so. Loughridge said nothing to the others, but it was clear

---

18   Unbeknownst to the commanding officers, Gallantry Head beacon had been shut down by French authorities.

to him that, without fathometer readings, Hickox could not nail down the time of crossing St. Pierre Bank with certainty. An hour ahead of schedule could mean that they were closing in on land.

He would have to estimate.

▼▲▼

2345 hours.

Bergeron climbed the ladder to the deck, wishing that he had his peacoat. He'd lost it somewhere in Boston while on liberty and he hadn't had time or money to buy another one[19] before shipping out. Now he was heading for watch on the fantail, the upper deck of the stern, in the dead of a blizzarding night wearing undressed blues and a Navy sweater. Lucky for him, a forgiving officer noticed.

"Hey, sailor, come here." The officer passed Bergeron his sheepskin jacket. "Drop it in the wardroom at the end of your watch."

Bergeron reddened, thanked the officer, and continued on his way. He stepped out on deck, careful where he planted his feet. The recruit he relieved flicked a frightened glance toward the rush of seas clobbering the stern, all but burying the *Truxtun*'s aft section. "Keep a sharp eye out for the *Pollux*," he hollered, face pinched with cold and nerves. He retched into the bucket lodged behind him and was gone.

Bergeron still felt nervy the first few minutes of night watch. The door closed behind the last watch, squeezing off the last smidgeon of low light, leaving him blind. He didn't like the sensation. Then, gradually, he began to make out the ship around him, the close, dark sky, and the wall of waves barrelling at him.

"Built like a Cuban cigar," his mates had laughingly labelled the *Truxtun*. Old. Reliable. In his briefing about the ship and watch duty, Egner had assured the recruits she could hold her own—in weather and

---

19   Rowsell, *Waves of Courage*, 154.

war. While Bergeron believed him, he couldn't help feeling edgy. A triple threat: wild weather, a wandering convoy, and German U-boats. The first wave of a U-boat campaign had already destroyed several dozen ships.[20] Just a few weeks ago, the *Alexander Hamilton,* a coast guard ship, was attacked by a German U-boat off the coast of Iceland. She was torpedoed on her starboard side, killing 26 men.[21] It wasn't just Iceland; U-boats could show up anywhere. Several had been spotted in the area they'd sailed the day before. Bergeron didn't want to think about it. Icebergs, too, were a threat. Last evening, on watch duty, they had navigated a heavy swath of slob ice that stretched for miles.

The steadily rising gale screeched through the rigging, bent on taking his legs out from under him. Driving sleet greasing the heaving deck made the slippery surface as precarious as navigating a patch of black ice. The North Atlantic regularly spawned heavy seas and rough weather, and tonight was as dire as she could deliver.

Maddocks, the OOD, on a turn outside, warned, "Stay sharp."

Bergeron stamped his feet, clenched and unclenched his hands, and squinted into the sleet. Somewhere out there between the *Truxtun* and *Wilkes,* the *Pollux* dodged along. Binoculars were useless in this weather.

Bergeron noticed his fellow watch mates staggering from bucket to bucket and couldn't help but feel pride that he had his stomach under control. He'd give anything for a drag. His superiors had drilled into the recruits that *dark adaptation* meant just that. No cigarettes; even a match could interfere with attaining night vision. He remembered one of his instructors saying that after exposure to the intensity of light required for reading, the eyes take 15 minutes to reach maximum dark sensitivity. Bergeron's job was to report on anything and everything out there: strange ships, land, any and all lights, icebergs, U-boats. And he needed sharp eyes to do it.

---

20   Adams, "Cold Comfort."
21   Rowsell, *Waves of Courage*, 41.

With the *Truxtun* under blackout, and the sky and sea black too, it was easy enough to conjure a U-boat lurking in the underbelly of every wave hurtling toward them—or an iceberg, like the one that had sunk the *Titanic*. From the start of the watch, either Newman, Hickox, or the OOD paced the wings continually peering over the side. There must be a reason why the officers, looking tense and preoccupied, darted from port to starboard wings and back inside like agitated bumblebees.

Had there been a warning from the *Wilkes*?

▼▲▼

Sailing blind? Maybe lost?

The voices were low. Phillips could hardly believe what he was hearing. Two ensigns, their foul weather gear piled in the corner, sat at the wardroom table. They nursed mugs of cocoa, hands still purple with cold. At the sideboard behind them, Phillips fussed with the hot plate. Had he heard right? Bracing himself against the heavy cupboard, he leaned in as close as he dared, aiming to catch the conversation.

"No soundings with the hand lead ... water too deep ... not at the speed we're sailing ..."

The ship rolled. Phillips secured the coffee pots and kneed the sideboard door shut just in time to keep the cutlery from clattering across the floor.

"... radio operator couldn't get any bearings on Cape Race ... or St. Pierre Island ... all static ..."

"... off course ... not a good position to be in."

"Especially on a night like this. No siree."

The ensigns drained their mugs, shouldered their gear, and left.

Phillips wiped up after them. Off course—that worried him. Some places didn't allow Black recruits ashore. Langston had told them that his first voyage on the *Truxtun* took him to Iceland. When the destroyer docked, the mess attendants couldn't take shore leave.[22] Iceland had strict laws preventing Blacks and other foreigners—such as his Filipino friend Tommy Dayo—from entering the country.[23]

Should he tell Langston that they might be off course? Maybe not. The boss wouldn't want him upsetting the mess crew. Turner would worry for sure, and Houston too. He headed along the passageway to his bunk. Best to keep it to himself. For now.

▼▲▼

Loughridge was OOD on the 0400-hour watch.

Before heading topside, he stopped by the wardroom for a coffee.

Newman filled him in: No data available, no bearings or soundings to fix their position, but the ship's distance from land, at this time, would be about 30 miles.[24]

A few minutes before 0345 hours, Loughridge arrived on the bridge. Hickox was catching a few hours shut-eye; Newman was back in the chart room. It was customary during night watch for the captain and the navigator to split the shift. Loughridge went to the chart and studied the ship's dead reckoning track. It looked to be well clear of land. Newman indicated the 0400-hour dead reckoning position. From the looks of it, Loughridge estimated that the nearest land would be no closer than 20 miles. He read the night orders and initialled the book. In compliance with the Navy mandate stating that the night watch must arrive 15 minutes before the start of the watch to allow for dark adaptation, he pulled up his collar and headed outside.

The *Truxtun* rode up a wall of black water, shivered atop, and dipped into a stomach-turning trough before rearing up to do it all

22   "Dead Reckoning: The Truxtun-Pollux Disaster," Maritime History Archive, https://www.mun.ca/mha/polluxtruxtun/index.php.
23   The United States routinely agreed to this order to secure rights to northern Atlantic air routes, to use Icelandic ports to ferry personnel, equipment, and supplies to Europe, and to maintain US Naval Air Station Keflavik for the defence of Iceland.
24   Brown, *Standing into Danger*, 100.

over again. Loughridge could barely make out the blurred forms of the lookouts braced against the wings, feet shuffling, arms flapping for warmth. They bore the brunt of the storm.

Not quite trusting the lookout abilities of the youngsters, Loughridge resolved to keep a close eye on them. Would they be able to spot the blur that was the *Pollux* through the dense wall of snow and sleet and spume? The weather raged. Winds revved up the seas. Visibility was down to 200 yards. The *Truxtun* rolled. They were caught up in a macabre mariner version of blind man's bluff. Loughridge willed the *Pollux* to come into view. No such luck.

He slipped back inside to the chart room. "Ready to relieve you, sir."

Maddocks replied, "Glad to see you." He read his notes to Loughridge: "Course 48 degrees true, speed 12 knots ... The navigator is in the chart house; we're steaming on 1 and 2 boilers. Visibility from about 200 to 300 yards, and getting worse."[25] He added, "And I had the gun crew move from the forward gun to guns number two and three. More shelter there. Less danger of being washed overboard."

Loughridge nodded and picked up the night watch log. According to the notes, at 0230 hours the navigator had ordered Maddocks to change course 1 degree to the right. Loughridge paused and re-read the note. He wondered about it, but then, in conditions such as these, corrections to the track were not unusual.

The sonar operator hustled in and out of the chart room, each report as bleak as the previous. Chief Fire Controlman Edward Petterson reported that the radioman had not been able to get a reading due to heavy static.

Newman looked ready to blow his top. "Tell him to keep taking bearings—and check to see that he does."

Petterson hurried back to the radio room. Loughridge followed and waited until the radioman finally got a bearing on Sable Island;

---

25   Brown, *Standing into Danger*, 101.

with concentrated static, the navigator didn't trust the reading. Out of options, Newman studied the chart.

Navigating a perilous coastline in foul weather, with two destroyers God knows how close, or distant, and unable to fix their position, was a watch even grimmer than Loughridge had anticipated. The fact that they were unable to make the *Wilkes* aware of the *Truxtun's* course change made matters worse. They'd have to use TBS (telephone between ships),[26] and with the threat of U-boats in the area all three ships were under strict orders regarding radio silence. Loughridge thought it a shame in these desperate conditions, but he didn't dare broach the subject with the navigator.

Star sights were still zip. The hand lead-line, good to 20 fathoms, was absolutely useless at this depth, and the *Truxtun*, lacking the navigational capability of the *Pollux* and *Wilkes*, was left to her own devices to manoeuvre as best she could.

Newman kept asking the radioman for RDF bearings, to no avail. Loughridge joined him on the port wing of the bridge. Both stared into the squally mess in front of them. Still there was no sight, or sound, of the *Pollux*.

The gun crew huddled around guns number two and three. The lookouts, caked in slush and sleet, stood at their posts.

Before Loughridge could utter a word, the quartermaster announced, "I saw a light spot in the sky, sir."[27]

Neither Newman nor Loughridge had seen it.

A split second later, a brooding scarp of ice and granite, massive in length and breadth and as grey as the murk enveloping it, loomed over them. It reared up to the sky a scant 200 yards from the *Truxtun's* bow. The officers, the gun watch, the deck crew, the lookouts all saw it.

Newman barked an order: "All engines stop! Full right rudder!"[28]

---

26   Short range transmitting voice radio.
27   Brown, *Standing into Danger*, 102.
28   Brown, *Standing into Danger*, 102.

Loughridge raced to the pilot house and rang up stop on the annunciator. He repeated Newman's order for full right rudder to the helmsman, who was already on it.

Returning outside, Loughridge shouted to the quartermaster, "Pass collision word."[29]

Newman took the annunciator and rang up, *Starboard back full.*[30]

The general alarm went off.

Amid the mesmerizing din of alarm bells, sirens, whistles, and shouted orders, the *Truxtun*, engines backing, swerved right about 10 degrees and veered away from the looming bluff. She lurched, scraped across something, maybe a submerged rock ledge.

The time: 0410 hours.

Unbeknownst to them, the *Truxtun* had struck ground only one minute after the *Wilkes*.

▼▲▼

The time: 0345 hours. Bergeron's shift was over, and not a minute too soon.

The 0400-hour watch was right on time for the quartermaster's briefing. He didn't envy those fellows just coming on watch duty. If anything, the seas were higher, the troughs deeper, the gale wilder than when his watch had begun. The *Truxtun* pitched about, a bobber tossing in the brine.

During the watch, a lifeboat had worked loose when the forward stay wire snapped and swung out over the side of the ship. Boatswain's Mate Andy Dusak and his deck crew had to suit up and hook it back in. A dicey job. Any one of them could have washed over the side; they came close enough. Bergeron admired their bravery. After the lifeboat was secured, the OOD sent them inside to warm up.

---

29   Brown, *Standing into Danger*, 102.
30   Brown, *Standing into Danger*, 102.

Bergeron was too cold to move with any speed. He vacated his post, walking stiffer than a rusted-up tin soldier. He couldn't even wrap his frozen claw around the railing of the ladder. He returned the jacket to the wardroom and stopped by the mess for a mug of cocoa before heading down the passageway to his cabin. It would take a gallon of hot cocoa to warm his vitals. He stopped to brace himself during a particularly bad roll. *The old girl was really outdoing herself tonight.* A slosh of cocoa here and there didn't matter much. There was water everywhere. Sea water always found a way in. It trickled down when the hatches opened, dripped off the seamen's gear, and condensed from the deck head.

All but Bergeron's own bunk was occupied. The cabin was loud with snores and grunts and ripe with the stench of sailors who hadn't showered since leaving port. Four-hour shifts didn't allow much time for personal grooming. Besides, a fellow didn't want to be caught in the head in the event of a U-boat hit—or an iceberg, for that matter—so many of his colleagues slept in their clothing. Not Bergeron. That was one thing about the Navy he hadn't gotten used to. Musty clothes and bedding were bad enough, but waking up in damp clothing was even worse. The cabin was freezing, as usual. Even so, he stripped down to his skivvies before diving into his bunk and burying his head under the covers. The *Truxtun*'s shuddering and groaning wouldn't keep him awake this morning. But his eyes had barely closed when he thought he felt the keel quiver.

He popped straight up. Was he dreaming?

And then she skidded. Ice. He knew it.

Emergency alarms blared. Bergeron shot out of bed, as did the others—six rogue projectiles in the dark cabin, until someone found the light switch. Tripping over bunk mates, he dived for his foul weather gear before his feet fully hit the deck and hauled it on over his skivvies in record drill time. Within seconds, Hickox ordered all hands on deck with life jackets on. The crew, in various states of emergency dress, pelted up the ladders. Bergeron snatched his life jacket and raced topside with them. *Cliffs? Could it be cliffs? Rearing up all around? Almost near enough to touch.*

He could hardly believe what his eyes were seeing.

They'd run aground.

▼▲▼

On the top bunk of five because of his junior rating, Phillips turned over in his mind the talk he'd overheard. Maybe it was all just blather.

Drifting off, he felt—he wasn't sure what—something like a shivering. A whole-ship tremor. Then the low, grinding sound of metal against rock. The *Truxtun* wasn't on wave-tops, Philips knew that much. He hit the deck of the cabin, along with his bunkmates, just as the alarms sounded. Like most of the crew, he'd slept with his clothes on. And he always kept his life jacket and shoes close in case of a possible torpedo hit. Falling over each other, in various states of dress, they spilled into the passageway, already clogged with shipmates. All hands made for the ladders, Phillips's long legs leaping four steps at a time. He burst out on deck, slipped on the icy surface,[31] and slid into the railing. Hauling himself up, he stared at the ghostly outline, stupefied.

Planted no more than 100 yards to starboard, through the murk of snow and spray, a mountain-sized ridge of rock reared up to the sky, the tip severed by cloud and fog. It wasn't blather after all. Phillips gripped the railing, eyes goggling, mouth agape.

Mercy. Mercy. Lord have mercy.

---

31   "Dead Reckoning."

CHAPTER 2
ST. LAWRENCE

Ena Farrell hurried down Church Lane.

Not at her usual pace, on account of the ice underfoot, but still faster than most could muster on a fine day.

The sky was heavy, brooding. Another day of unsettled weather. A wicked gale whipped around Cape Chapeau Rouge and into the harbour. She was used to that, but she could have done without the squall of sleet, sharp on her face. The fresh smudge of ashes Father Thorne had dabbed on her forehead as he intoned the familiar Lenten prayer "Remember, man, you are but dust" must be a runny smear by now.[32]

A fitting day for Ash Wednesday. The beginning of Lent. Forty days of fasting and offering-up leading up to Easter. Ena hadn't eaten breakfast so that she could take Communion at Mass. That took care of fasting. On the spot, she offered up this awful weather and, as her brother would say, gut-foundering hunger. There. Both done for the day. And it wasn't yet 10 a.m. She chuckled at what her mother would make of her cheekiness as she passed the causeway and speed-walked down the harbour, catching herself mid-slip more than once.

Last April, shortly after her 22nd birthday, she'd graduated with honours from a full-fledged business course at Mercy Convent Commercial Academy in St. John's.[33] Now a general office worker at the new business in town, Hollett Sons & Co. Ltd., she certainly didn't want to be late for work—even though the storekeeper, Mr. Hollett,

---

32   Ena Farrell Edwards, *St. Lawrence and Me* (St. John's, NL: Flanker, 2001), 87.
33   Edwards, *St. Lawrence and Me*, 26.

HARD AGROUND | 27

knew that she was getting the ashes this morning.

The straggle of churchgoers returning home from Mass dwindled, but a bit farther along a string of vehicles headed up the road to Iron Springs toward the mine. Travelling at a good clip.

▼▲▼

As Alan Farrell's helper, 19-year-old Gus Etchegary got to drive around in a mine truck. His buddies envied him. Not that there was far to go in the outport[34] settlement of St. Lawrence, population maybe 1,000 since the mines had started up. The mine workers were used to negotiating the rutted dirt roads by horse cart in summer and sleigh in winter. All the supplies and freight needed within the community and for the operation of the fluorspar mines (Black Duck, Director, Hare's Ears, Iron Springs, and a few others) were brought in by coastal steamer.[35]

Alan and Gus had put miles on the old truck driving to and from the mines picking up, loading, and unloading equipment and parts (pumps, pipes, drills, and the like). They were in the truck about to leave the mill with a load of drums and some timber—Gus's father was the mill superintendent there and his older brother, Theo, the chemist—when the office door burst open. Theo emerged, waved them down, two coils of rope in his hand: a 6-thread and an 18-thread. He threw them in the back and climbed into the cab.

Before Gus could ask what was going on, Theo relayed the gist of a phone call he had just received from Rube Turpin, the mechanical operations supervisor for Iron Springs. A ship was ashore in Chambers Cove. A sailor had scaled the cliff and made it to the mine. It didn't sound good, Rube had said. Alan shifted the old dump into gear. The

---

34   A coastal settlement, outside the chief port of St. John's. *Dictionary of Newfoundland English* s.v. "outport."

35   Rennie Slaney, *More Incredible than Fiction: The True Story of the Indomitable Men and Women of St. Lawrence, Newfoundland from the Time of Settlement to 1965* (Montreal: Confederation of National Trade Unions/La Confédération des Syndicats Nationaux, 1975), 28.

short stretch of road was studded with potholes that compounded its rattles and shakes, but Alan got them to the mine even faster than his usual breakneck speed.

When they arrived, there were no men about. Theo said that Pop and mine captain Rennie Slaney had pulled the miners off their shift and sent them to the cove. They'd shut down production for the day[36] and had already contacted the acting manager, Howard Farrell, and advised him of the morning's events. Theo went to the warehouse for more heavy rope. Alan jumped out of the cab and followed. Gus felt around under the seat for his cap, grabbed a coil of half-inch rope from the back of the truck, and then lit out for the path leading to the cove. Blotches of black oil littered the broken trail.

Adrenaline pumping, he took off at a run.

▼▲▼

Ash Wednesday was a Day of Obligation. If you could do it at all, you were expected to attend Mass.

Clara Tarrant had two little ones underfoot. She'd sent the older ones off to get the ashes, and the four of them would soon be traipsing home for breakfast before going back for school. She planned on going to evening Mass. She heard a tap on the door; a young fellow stood on the porch step, with Aunt Mary Jackman right behind him, both talking a mile a minute.

"Holy Mother of God—*ashore*? In this weather? God help them."

The young fellow said, "It's pretty bad out there. We need women to help with the survivors. Some are in rough shape. Can you come to the mine house?" He gulped a mouthful of air. "The men on the morning shift are all gone to the cove and the ones just home from the night shift are being picked up to go back and help."

---

36   Linden MacIntyre, *The Wake: The Deadly Legacy of a Newfoundland Tsunami* (Toronto: HarperCollins, 2019), 189.

By the time Ella and Carmel burst into the porch, Clara had her coat on and was halfway out the door with Aunt Mary, calling instructions for the two older girls to look after the little ones and do the breakfast dishes and tidy up the rest of the house too.[37]

Patrick, Clara's husband, worked at Hare's Ears Mine. She wondered if he had heard anything.

---

37   Carmel Turpin (Clara's daughter), telephone conversation with author, October 8, 2020.

CHAPTER 3
USS TRUXTUN

In the chilling predawn of 0415 hours, the brutal crag appeared to lean over the *Truxtun*.

Loughridge felt that he could almost reach out and touch it. How could this be? He couldn't wrap his mind around it. Just half an hour ago, the charts showed them to be 20 miles from land. Twenty miles! Yet, here they were.

Hickox and his officers darted to the bridge in a scramble to generate a plan of action. A hasty inspection revealed that the *Truxtun* was aground forward with her bow snagged on the ledge. A hundred yards to starboard, a vertical wall of rock stretched upward some 200 feet to rim the entire cove; portside, the northern rim drifted even higher, 300 feet of straight-up rock. The fact that she was on an even keel and her stern floating free gave the officers hope. Somewhat sheltered in the cove, the ship still jockeyed on sizable swells.

The large searchlight was dead. The smaller light's paltry 3-inch beam played over the icy face of the bluff and swept the length of the *Truxtun*: forward, aft, starboard, port. The ship lay between two hulking rocks. One, layered with ice, reared out of the spume close to her starboard side; on her left, closer to shore, a matching one perched amid breakers that resembled the open maw of a steel trap.

The patch of light that had been spotted earlier off the port quarter still wigwagged eerily back and forth. It seemed to be a reflection of a ship's searchlight. No one commented. They had other concerns. After appraising their plight, Hickox and his officers determined that the vessel was not caught hard. Hickox ordered both engines full astern. The crew held their collective breath. The engines, in reverse, screeched. The ship juddered, backed off a foot, and another. Then, with the bow acting as a pivot, high winds and heavy seas swung her stern swung strongly to port and onto the clutter of rocks, tearing off screws, ripping open her hull, and spewing a heavy bleed of fuel oil into the cove.[38]

The crew, thrown about, hung on to whatever they could grab as heavy swells walloped the ship, ramming her on the rocks, the terrible sounds echoing tenfold off the cliffs. Loughridge picked himself up. The starboard anchor was dropped to stabilize the bow. Hickox ordered Loughridge to alert the *Wilkes* by TBS. No response. An attempt was then made to signal by the small searchlight. No reply. Fearful of revealing the position of a US Navy combat ship, Hickox would not break radio silence.

Loughridge stepped outside and followed the searchlight's dim beam. They'd need a plan to tackle that scarp. But first, they would have to make it ashore—in 5-foot waves, a hefty gale, and intermittent blizzard conditions. He wasn't optimistic. The beam skimmed the water's edge, and played over the southeast end of the coastline, where there appeared to be a slight bit of beach already edged in black Bunker C crude. That strip of land might make all the difference.

Hickox ordered: "Have the crew dress warmly and bring all blankets topside before proceeding to their abandon-ship positions."

In the aft engine room, Maddocks, the engineer's assistant, tried every trick he knew to keep the pumps and generators going. In spite of his efforts, the machinery worked loose, breaking off at the foundations. The keel, bilge plates, and the frames were buckling and cracking.[39] Pumps could not keep up with the incoming water. Rocks had smashed in the portside. The trickle grew to a flood. Loughridge,

---

38   Brown, *Standing into Danger*, 108.
39   Brown, *Standing into Danger*, 109.

who also wore the hat of Torpedo Officer, pounded down the ladder. He grabbed a spanner wrench and with Sloan Jones, Tactical Weapons Operator, and Edward McInerney, Fireman 2nd Class, set all the depth charges on safe.[40] There was nothing left to do but retreat.

Hickox ordered: "Secure the boilers. Abandon aft engineering spaces."

The steam was let out of the boilers to prevent them from blowing up, and all light and heat were cut off aft. Gradually, the *Truxtun* listed to starboard. Ferocious breakers hove her high and, just as suddenly, slammed her back down on the rocks. She still had power from the forward engine room, which operated the searchlight, but there was little they could do until daylight.

Hickox ordered Radioman Lovira Legett to transmit an emergency distress signal, but before he could do so they received a distress call from the *Wilkes*: "*Wilkes* aground entrance Placentia Bay. Stand by us if possible."

Hickox himself radioed the *Truxtun*'s response: "We are on the rocks. Dog tanks holed. Both props useless and rudder out of whack.

"Am abandoning ship."[41]

Hickox ordered that abandon-ship procedures be set in motion.

Bergeron was part of a crew assigned the job of piling weighted bags of confidential material on the well deck in preparation for going ashore. He bobbed his head toward the searchlight beam sweeping the cliff. "The line-throwing guns won't get anywhere near that," he said to the seaman stacking bags next to him.

Once that was done, Bergeron helped gather all the wire cable and 3-inch manila line they could scrounge up and piled it on the forecastle. Hickox had ordered his officers to run a lifeline ashore; they would need the rope to make it to land—and maybe even to scale that cliff.

---

40   Stewart, "Naval Disaster in Newfoundland," Reader comment, posted September 1, 2016, 9:16 p.m. There is no information available that Loughridge was with Jones and McInerney as they set the depth charges on safe, but, as torpedo officer, it is probable that he was there.

41   Brown, *Standing into Danger*, 109.

Hickox wondered where the flagship and the *Pollux* were.[42] They should be here, not off on some zigzag. Every ship in the Navy should be steaming to their aid. Instead, the *Truxtun* was on her own—impaled on the rocks—with not a Navy ship in sight. Skedaddling back and forth topside, too fired up to feel the cold, he wondered instead about the situation below deck.

Some had ducked below to gather personal items such as wallets and pictures before the passageways flooded with water.

▼▲▼

The crew, in various states of emergency dress, rumbled up the ladders. Phillips hurried to his abandon-ship station.

The large searchlight seemed to be out of commission. The smaller beam glimmered through the muddle of hard weather. Just off the starboard bow, Phillips could see heavy seas surging toward a heavily iced cliff. The situation appeared serious, but not disastrous.

The rest of the crew seemed to feel the same way; no one was panicking. Phillips heard them talk: Land was near enough. The ship was upright—mostly. And Hickox was rated by his crew as one of the best. With daybreak, the Navy would come to their rescue and either tow them to Argentia for repairs or take them aboard, if it came to that.

Langston arrived shortly and ordered the mess crew to bring every blanket they could find and stash them on the deck just aft of the lifeboat station. Back and forth they hurried, adding to the pile.

Egner was at the lifeboat station, his crew bunched around him. Phillips cocked an ear. "The forward stay wire is busted," Egner told his men, referring to the lifeboat that had been secured inboard earlier. His voice rose above the racket of ship and wind. "Captain says to get her in position to lower."

---

42   The crew of the *Truxtun* remained unaware that the *Wilkes* and the *Pollux* were also aground.

Phillips watched as Egner shouted, "Like this," waving his arms to show them. "We have to push the bow out and forward, or the stern won't clear the aft davit."[43]

Phillips eyed the lifeboat and davit. It could be done—with exact timing. On the count of three, the crew swung the bow out and forward. Frozen in position, the men waited until the ship rolled to starboard. Hindered by biting sleet in their faces and the slippery deck, they manoeuvred the lifeboat forward. But before the two aft seamen could get the stern out, the *Truxtun* rolled to port. The lifeboat swung back in, banging against number four smokestack. Try number two failed. As did number three. On the fourth attempt, the boat veered back and crashed against the same smokestack, gouging a sizable hole in its side.[44] The crew stepped out of the wind and took a breather.

Egner reported the loss of the lifeboat to Hickox and returned to his crew with orders to launch the gig. Their chances of lowering it were slimmer than they'd been with the lifeboat. If the men manoeuvred the gig into position for lowering, it would hang directly over one of the huge rocks. One of the sailors grabbed the line in an attempt to ease the boat halfway down the side, to see if the seas would take it clear of the rock. The waves lifted the gig and lobbed her down on the jagged slab. The gig snapped in two, like a piece of kindling.

Done in, the crew joined the seamen taking shelter behind the galley deck. They dug into the tub of apples and oranges the cook had put out for breakfast. Phillips, having finished gathering blankets, trailed along behind them. He thought of his friend, James Foster, safe aboard the *Pollux*. Lucky duck. Phillips would have a story for him when they docked in Argentia.

The canteen chief doled out candy.

---

43   A small crane on board a ship, especially one of a pair for suspending or lowering a lifeboat.
44   Brown, *Standing into Danger*, 110.

"You'll want us to pay up once we make shore," the sailors ribbed the chief.

Phillips sucked on his candy, enjoying the teasing. With the rising tide though, the jokes petered out. The gale doubled down on the *Truxtun*; it savaged the ship, dashing her against the rocks. Punishing waves rushed the galley deck and dumped barrels of numbing sea water on the men huddled there. Phillips prodded the foot of a seaman lying in a heap next to him. Getting no response, he nudged the man's shoulder. His dull eyes blinked. He was still alive. Philips hauled him to his feet, urging him to keep moving.

Some sailors, topside without foul weather gear, shrouded their shoulders and necks with blankets; others wrapped blankets around their heads and tugged them tight to the chin. Some had already succumbed and lay lifeless on the deck. Still others hobbled around shoeless. The soles of their bare feet, skinned on the steel deck, left their footprints in blood.[45] One sailor removed a dead man's shoes and put them on his own bleeding feet. Phillips couldn't blame him. Still, it was a hard thing to watch.

A few men decided to strike out for the beach. One jumped. Several others leaped after him. Phillips and his shipmates watched them struggling to swim through the debris. Willed them to make shore. Sailors on deck lobbed empty apple and orange crates over the side in hopes that their mates could grab them and drift or swim ashore. Winds and flood tide claimed the crates; their mates, swallowed by the surf. Then, a gigantic wave snatched them up, bore their pitiful carcasses 100 feet up the cliff, and launched them at the scarp before dropping them to the rocks below. Phillips, Langston, Turner, Houston, Dayo— the whole mess crew—watched in horror, buckled. Sucker-punched. They stepped back into the shelter of the ship, recoiling in anguish.

Phillips prayed that they would get off the ship soon.

---

45   Adams, "Cold Comfort."

▼▲▼

The time: 0630 hours. The lifeboat and the gig were gone.

Hickox ordered the inflated life rafts to be launched. All six—three starboard, three portside—appeared to be sound. The crew knew the drill. Suspended above the main deck outside the rigging, the life rafts would be lowered into the water and held alongside the hull to allow sailors to drop into them.

The operation, normally executed in open water, was trickier in heavy seas with the ship listing above a cache of rocks. Number One Starboard Life Raft met the same fate as the captain's gig—smashed on the same massive rock. Out of commission. Numbers Two and Three Starboard Life Rafts ricocheted off the rock and knocked against the ship. The crew tried pulling Number Two around the stern to the bow. Waves tore the lines out of their hands. The sea took Number Three before they could step away.

With the three starboard life rafts gone, the crew turned to the port life rafts. All three overturned the second they hit the breakers. Under orders from Ensign Howard Taylor, sailors battled seas and gale to haul the upside-down rafts to the port bow. "Easier to load the men there in preparation for landing," Taylor said.

The men tried repeatedly to upright the gyrating life rafts, with no success. Loughridge looked on in horror as one sailor jumped overboard to try and heave the raft upright. He thrashed about in the waves, panic-stricken.

Taylor shouted, "Quick, get me a lifeline!"

The line was speedily attached to his life jacket, and he dived in. But the sailor had already been swept away. The crew hauled Taylor aboard and someone led him inside for dry clothes. The men, more determined than ever, laboured to right the life rafts.

Seamans arrived on the scene. "They're going about it wrong," he said to the officers supervising the crew's futile attempts. He called to the men, "Get the grappling hooks. Aim them for the far side of the rafts. When they connect, pull the lines. That should upright the rafts."

The hooks appeared. After a few tries, the first portside life raft was righted to the sound of cheers from the crew. The chief petty officer reported to Hickox that Number One Portside Life Raft was ready.[46]

Breathing easier, Loughridge turned his attention from the life rafts to making landfall. Daylight had come later than usual, held back by the weather. He trained the binoculars shoreward and sharpened the focus for a better look at that speck of strand he was sure he'd seen earlier. There it was, the image blurred, but unmistakable even through the haze.

They must make that strip of shingle.

▼▲▼

Bergeron was relieved to see the end of night—until the light revealed what they faced.

In the squally half-light, between blasts of sleet or snow or hail, or the collusion of all three, he scanned the coastline. The *Truxtun* had brought up in a rocky crook of a cove, a slight curve of cliff hardly more than the blade of a scythe in an otherwise angular coastline. Even in the shelter of the cove, the hard weather was hindersome. Bergeron was used to snow and wind. But not this. The North Atlantic howler, raging in full swagger, veered around, breezed up from the south, skimmed the crests off surly breakers and slung them against the cliffs. A crop of rocks slathered in ice and fuel oil littered the sluice between the *Truxtun* and the cove. Bergeron didn't relish the idea of having to row or swim through that. They might not have to. The *Truxtun* looked to be parked between those rocks. Maybe they could ride out the storm until the seas abated. Bergeron had seen Hickox and his officers

---

46   Brown, *Standing into Danger*, 154.

training their binoculars on the far end of the little cove. Sure enough, there was a sliver of beach. And he was almost certain that, above it, he could make out a line of fencing. He pointed it out to his mates. "See there on the far end, past the overhang, where the cliff is not as steep?"

Eyeballs strained upward. The boys agreed. "Yep, that's a fence!" They echoed each other, voices rising in triumph. "Man, there must be a farm up there."

"All we have to do is get to the beach," Bergeron said, matter of fact.

The life raft crew had been working on righting the port rafts. As Bergeron staggered along the sloping deck, he peered over the side. All three life rafts were upright; the sailors who engineered the feat were taking a breather. Another team grabbed coils of 3-inch manila line from the growing heap.

"What are you doing with that?" Bergeron asked.

A sailor explained, "The life raft going over will tow a line attached to the ship. So we can haul it back."

Another, reaching for a coil, cut in, "This heavier rope will be attached to the lighter one. To establish a lifeline, see?"

Bergeron nodded. "Who's taking it ashore?"

The sailor shrugged. "Whoever goes, it'll be a devil to paddle."

"Have you ever crewed one?" Bergeron asked.

"Yep," the seaman replied. "Once, in boot camp. Man, those inflated life rafts are hard enough to paddle in calm harbour water."

"How come?" Bergeron asked.

"You never been in one?"

Bergeron shook his head.

"Well," the fellow explained, "the sides are rounded and inflated, right?"

Bergeron nodded.

"And there's grating on the bottom. You must have seen that." He didn't wait for Bergeron to respond. "A rope net secures the grating to the inflated sides. When you board, the raft sinks a foot or more. You end up standing or sitting in water." He added, "Normally, the crew sits on the sides to paddle."

Bergeron nodded. "That wouldn't be so good in these seas."

"No, siree," the sailor added, as he made off with the rope.

Bergeron heard someone call for Egner. Hickox wanted to see him. All ears perked up. The men followed Egner to see what was up. Hickox wanted a man to take a life raft ashore. Egner was just the man to do it.

With no hesitation, Egner nodded in the affirmative. "Yes, sir."

Hickox, looking at the men gathered around, said, "Pick your crew."

Egner turned to the men. The life raft could hold 15. No one looked anxious to go, and he didn't blame them. Then, Seaman 2nd Class James Fex stepped forward.

Egner nodded. "I think Fex and I can make it, sir."

On deck, there was considerable excitement at the prospect. Bergeron could feel the lift among the men. A surge of energy swept the deck. A stirring of hope. The raft was readied. Rations, water, a first aid kit, and paddles were stowed. Egner, followed by Fex, a bruiser of a sailor, slid down the ropes into the twisting life raft.[47] They sank, just like the seaman had said.

The port railing was lined off with their watching mates.

Just when Bergeron thought they would disappear under the barrage of foaming surf, the raft, riding a steep angle, bobbed to the surface. Egner and Fex were still aboard. Kneeling on the bottom grating, the two men aimed for open sea in an effort to clear the rocks; the waves would propel them toward the beach.

Forward, back, and sideways they volleyed. The crew could barely stand to watch. The raft, a heavy contraption, grew more cumbersome, caked thick with oil and weightier still with the drag of the line, a black wick gathering layer upon layer of black gel.

---

47   Rowsell, *Waves of Courage*, 49.

Egner and Fex strained toward shore, the men on deck straining with them. Their paddles were as useless as toothpicks in a tempest. Still, they seemed to make marginal headway. Closer. Almost there. There was a collective intake of breath from the crew as a gigantic roller, coming from behind Egner and Fex, hefted the raft high, and shoved it through the surf to the edge of the beach. It had taken 30 tortuous minutes to make shore. The deck erupted in roars of relief. A big fellow next to Bergeron shot up in the air and landed square on his foot. Bergeron responded by jumping on his back. Their ship may have been broken and on the rocks, but the crew's spirits were riding high.

After another 30 minutes, Egner and Fex signalled that they were ready to haul in the 3-incher that the crew had attached to the lifeline. Bergeron could see why it had taken so long. Having wrestled massive waves to get to the beach, Egner and Fex then had to haul ashore the heavy hawser, wrapped in debris. They must be half-dead. Every 50 feet or so, they stopped pulling for a break of about 10 minutes. While waiting, the seamen at the railing jiggled and swung their arms to ward off the raw chill.

Repeatedly, the *Truxtun*'s signalman waved his flags, signalling them to hurry.

Finally, Egner and Fex signalled that the lifeline was secure. There was no line-up for the second life raft. The crew had witnessed the hell Egner and Fex had endured. Even with a lifeline to haul themselves across hand over hand, no one was eager to volunteer; they would rather take their chances with the ship. Petterson, given the task of supervising the landing, finally managed to round up a few.

Hickox and his officers stood in a huddle. Making his way toward them, Bergeron, half-dressed and soaking wet, volunteered for the second life raft. Newman gave the okay.[48] Finally, a total of 10 men agreed to go. Each man was ordered to take a blanket with him. Boarding proved tricky with rope and raft wildly out of sync—the

---

48   Rowsell, *Waves of Courage*, 154.

rope whisked about on a cruel wind, the raft weaponized by the seas. Bergeron jumped aboard, blanket tucked under his arm, and hung on for the ride of his life.

Coated in crude, the lifeline had thickened to a hawser and a half. Steeling his rubbery arms, Bergeron yanked the line in tandem with the beefy seaman in front of him. Most of the time he kept the pace. From time to time, he peered around the fellow's back to track their headway. Bergeron pulled, grunted, pulled harder, grunted louder. He wanted to wipe his face, rub the salt from his eyes, and stretch his right leg. He could do none of it. Ten more pulls. Then 10 more. Halfway through the next round, the raft grazed bottom.

Bergeron leaped overboard and touched bottom up to his waist in the surf. He clung to the side of the raft; he wasn't going to be swept out to sea at this stage. Ice fringed the tips of his Navy brush cut. A vicious gale drilled the side of his head, his fingers and toes felt like frozen sausages. He and his shipmates, clumsy from the life-sucking cold, scrabbled up the shingle beach. "We made it in 15 minutes," the chief shouted over the roar of the surf.

They dragged the slimed-up raft out of the surf.

A tarry scum of Bunker C crude, a foot deep, clotted the cave.

▼▲▼

Hickox ordered a towline attached to the remaining raft.

Phillips watched.

The rescue team had piled cable and rope on the forecastle. Phillips and Turner had the job of keeping the stocks separate and orderly as the raft crew hurried back and forth grabbing coils to take ashore.

Turner said, "What if this is Iceland? Only whites are allowed ashore there."

Iceland was the last place on Phillips's mind. He squinted through the weather and seas toward the fogged-in beach. "We're not ashore yet. Put it out of your head."

One thing he knew for certain. He and the mess crew would go last. After the white sailors.

Anything could happen by then.

▼▲▼

Two life rafts had made it to shore intact; the second raft was on its way back to the ship.

Loughridge watched it fight through the sludge and wreckage in a clumsy tug-of-war between ship and sea. Hickox couldn't wait any longer. The remaining raft was already righted. Once the crew attached a towline, it was ready to go ashore.

The storm seemed to have eased. At any rate, the sleeting had stopped.

The *Truxtun*, though, was taking a licking. Monstrous breakers barrelling into the cove picked her up and rammed her down on the ragged crop of rocks surrounding her starboard and port. She listed farther to starboard. Bone-jarring thuds threw the sailors off-kilter as they careened along her slanting deck.

Hickox summoned Loughridge to take the next raft to the beach— to supervise the landing and to take charge of the men ashore. On Loughridge's instructions, the sailors dropped from the forecastle into the raft. The raft hefted up and joggled on a wave-top almost level with the *Truxtun*'s deck before falling at a stomach-turning speed into a deep trough. Gloves or bare hands caked in crude, they strained for leverage on the greasy cable as they struck out for shore, eyes trained on the strip of shingle.

Inch by inch, the rope fell behind them.

▼▲▼

On shore, Bergeron checked out the cove.

The sheer cliffs were sheeted in sinister ice. He could see no shelter. The wind, the waves, more vicious away from the shelter of the ship. Half the beach was already under water, with flood tide licking at their heels. Where would they go?

Bergeron wasn't waiting around to find out. He, Petterson, and a few others scouted the shoreline. Bergeron headed across the shingle to the far south end of the cove, where there was more slope and the cliffs not as steep. However, to get to that slope they would have to first climb over a rocky outcrop at the end of the beach. Bergeron crawled on all fours over the icy boulders and down the other side, checking out one way, then another, before settling on a route.

Barehanded, using his knife as an ice pick, he stabbed at the frozen ground, crosscutting a path up the heavily iced slope. The others had fallen behind. Only Petterson, shouldering a light line, trailed after him.[49] Shards fell back on him like a silver thaw. On hands and knees, they clawed their way up, tacking according to the incline, hugging the rock as they neared the top.

Never once did they let themselves think they could slip or fall back on the rocks below.

▼▲▼

Phillips watched the third raft pitch about in possessed seas. The men aboard—only five this time—grabbed the lifeline.

He should have gone. Most at the railing figured they'd have as good a chance in a barrel. Langston and his mess crew agreed. The third raft reached shore and the five men aboard plunged into the surf.

---

49   Rowsell, *Waves of Courage*, 155.

Above the hurrays and cheers, Maddocks, who had been watching the raft's progress through binoculars, shouted, "Hey, look!" He waved his binoculars toward the cliff. "See over there ... It's Chief Petterson and Bergeron going up the cliff!"

Phillips screwed up his eyes. Sure enough, at the far end of the beach, on the side of the slope were two men. Black etchings on the snow-crusted scarp. Creeping upward. Crookedly. In micro-moves. There were more cheers and yells. For sure, help would soon be here. There was talk again of the fence at the top and the farm they hoped was nearby. Buoyed up by the sight of Bergeron and Petterson, the men looked to the clifftop expectantly. And waited. Their excitement was short-lived. When the two disappeared over the top of the cliff, and nothing else appeared to be happening, the men's attention returned to their own wretchedness.

The only raft able to return was still lumbering back to the ship along the lifeline. Phillips scrutinized its progress. The lifeline was balled up in crude and junk that had been tossed overboard. The raft flipped when the sea snared it. Again, when the wind took it. The crew on the forecastle laboured to bring it alongside. Finally, they reined it in.

The call went out for volunteers. Turner was not boarding; he would take his chances with the ship. Besides, if that beachhead was Iceland, he wouldn't be permitted to set foot ashore anyway. Houston feared they could be lynched. Turner nodded. Dayo was not about to leave either.[50] It was hell out there. He trusted the Navy to save him from it.

Phillips counted 10 men. The raft could hold 15. There was room. Not like they would be taking seats from white sailors. "There's space for us," he told his pals.

But Langston, Houston, Turner, and Dayo could not work themselves up to it.

Phillips hopped aboard.

---

50   Lanier Phillips was the only Black man to survive. The other Black crew members, Henry G. Langston, Earl Houston, and Billy Gene Turner, as well as Tomas Dayo (Filipino), lost their lives.

▼▲▼

Finally, the raft Loughridge crewed scraped across rock and pebbles, a sound more melodious to Loughridge's eardrums than the tunings of the Andrews Sisters.

They had made it. Then Loughridge's foot snagged in the netting, and he nosedived into the flotsam. He was dragged under the surf headfirst. And held there. Then he felt arms pulling him to the surface. Egner and Fex worked his foot free and lugged him up the beach, coughing oil and belching sea water.

Loughridge croaked a grateful thank you. Quickly recovering, he took charge. "When the next raft lands," he said to Egner, "we have to tie the two together and hitch them to the hawser, so that both rafts can be pulled back to the ship at the same time."

Waist deep in the frigid surf, sailors attached the two rafts to the lifeline and signalled the *Truxtun* to haul them in.

Fifty feet out, the rafts twisted around the line, tight as a bobber to a pole.

▼▲▼

Bergeron's every thought, every heart thump homed in on that faint line of fence, and the farmhouse that might be beyond it.

Or a barn at least. He and Petterson hauled themselves over the lip and sprawled, spreadeagled, hearts thumping, chuffing gulps of arctic air. Their senses, dulled by the cold and the climb, shut down at the sight before them. Not a single tree blotted the barrens.

No farmhouse. No barn.

The fence they had hoped would mean safety—and all that went with it—went nowhere. It penned snowdrifts, and nothing else. Bergeron felt the desolation to his core.

To their right, the land dipped down to a gully. Through an

onslaught of sleet, they spied a shed. Looping the rope around a lump of ice, in case their shipmates would need it later, they slid down the hard crust of snow, their oily clothes as good as greased runners. The rough shed stood on low posts with a slight peak to the roof. No door. Inside was dark and deadly cold, but it did offer some shelter. Petterson, exhausted, slumped down on a pile of hay.

The shack.

Bergeron stayed just long enough to catch his breath. He had to find help. Not heeding the stiff gale assaulting him, he ran. The hillside was steeper than it looked, and covered in ice and snow. He slipped, fell, and slid 10 or more feet before he managed to grab a prickly bush and anchor himself. Ice sent him sprawling one minute and the next he sank to his thighs in snowdrifts.

Eyes peeled for some sign of habitation, he broke a ragged trail, hoping that he was heading toward a village. The squall of sleet had abated, leaving a sullen sky. A slight flit of light caught his eye. Fighting fatigue, he stumbled on, as fast as he could.

There it was again. Flickering. Intermittent through the mist and fog. A bit farther on the spectral shape of a building emerged through the mess of weather. Tallish? An odd shape. And seeming to be attached to the light? About a mile off, he figured.

The slope of land eased.

But directly ahead, and blocking his way, was a brook full to the brim and nearly mad as the seas. He skidded alongside the bank until he came to a rickety wooden bridge, slippery as an ice rink and heaved at a steep angle. Without testing it, he blundered across, muzzy eyes glued on that building, that light, a wan glimmer through the blur of fog and cloud and snow. Closer, the light seemed to be on top of a frame, the building ... maybe a mine site? He closed the distance, barely able to keep going. Could see a figure coming toward him.

Felt the strength of a man link arms with his, helping him toward the building.

Phillips spilled out of the raft and onto the beach.[51] He forced himself upright, despite his wobbly legs.

He witnessed in horror the two rafts snarl around the lifeline. And watched, eyes locked on Egner and Fex and others battling the waves to work the line free. For all their efforts, the line wouldn't budge. Could their luck get any worse? It could. A few minutes later, the *Truxtun*'s signalman sent a message to Signalman Bo Parkerson on shore, who relayed it to the officer: Untie the lifeline to the ship.

Untie the lifeline?

51   Meg Rowsell and Wayde Rowsell, "USS Pollux & Truxtun Incident 18 February 1942," See and Hear, The National World War II Museum, New Orleans, February 18, 2012, http://www.nww2m.com/2012/02/uss-pollux-truxtun-incident/.

Officer Loughridge directed Egner and Fex to carry out the order. Phillips knew that they had no say in the matter: orders were orders. But they didn't look happy about it.

"It's the only thing to do," the officer said. "It's a setback, but it will allow the rafts to be hauled back to the ship; they can then make another attempt to reach shore."

To Phillips, it was worse than a setback. He waited with the crew for action from the *Truxtun*, expecting to see the rafts close the distance to the ship—however slowly. Nothing happened. Then the *Truxtun*'s signalman waved his flags: the lifeline was snagged on the bottom of the cove; they were unable to pull the rafts back to the ship.

The men swore.

Any hope Phillips still nursed drained out of him, pooling in the crud around his feet. There was no raft for his mess buddies to come ashore; they were stranded on a sinking ship, their only lifeline balled up in a snarl halfway between ship and shore. Phillips had shared a cabin with the four men and worked with them every day. They were like family. He wished that he had tried harder to convince them to board the raft. It was worse than gut-wrenching to think that they might not make it.

"Well, men, there's nothing more to be done here," Loughridge said, as he scrutinized the run of cliffs cupping the mingy cove. "We need to find shelter."

Egner pointed up the beach. "There's a notch in the cliff, just a cranny, over there, to the north."

"On your feet, men," the officer ordered.

With Egner in the lead, they footslogged up the beach. Phillips was having a hard time turning his back on the ship; he couldn't help but feel that he was turning his back on his buddies too. With roughly 20 men jammed inside the cranny, they had to literally take turns breathing. The deadly cold was almost worse than being in the open air. Their wet clothes had already frozen stiff. Fingers and toes deadened as the numbing seeped into hands and feet. The rock face looming over them was unscalable, any thought of climbing it cancelled out by the sheer slope and heavy wrap of ice. And adding to their hardship, the winds had shifted, pushing heavy seas directly into the cove.

Loughridge nagged them: Keep moving. Move your limbs. Follow the others up the cliff. But in their exhausted, frozen state, there was no heart to their scuffs and shuffles.

Egner announced, "I'm not staying here to freeze to death." He and a half-dozen seamen struck out for the far end of the beach where the others had gone up. Phillips, energized by the notion of finding help, trekked after them. Anything was better than that crack in the rock. Already, bodies were washing ashore: men who had tried to swim or who were swept overboard by the waves. Phillips looked away, the lump in his throat a lead ball lodged against his windpipe.

The men tramped after Egner, checking the slope for where the others had gone. Nothing. Bergeron and Petterson had not sprouted wings; they had climbed up somewhere. The men clawed their way over the jags of rimed-up rock jutting out from the cliff at the far end of the shingle.

Phillips pointed to a gully and called to Egner, "I think this might be where they climbed up."

Egner was standing at the foot of a ravine with a trench running down the middle. It was steep, but it might have enough of a slant for them to make it up without too much danger. Phillips went first. Flat to the slope, he scratched finger- and toeholds in the rimy gravel, sliding back almost as much as he made headway. Grit shredded his palms and chiselled under the flesh; limbs splayed like frog legs seized before he was halfway up. Head bowed to the effort, banging knees and elbows on icy juts, hands frozen claws, he pulled himself upward. Close behind him, Egner, also plastered against the scarp, scraped a trail on elbows and knees.

"We're almost up," Phillips called back.

At the top, the gully ended, swallowed by a slab of straight-up granite close to 5 feet high and sheeted in ice. Phillips paused and looked around. Seeing no other way, he stretched his lanky frame up the slab, grabbed whatever he could, and hoisted himself over the rim. He crawled away from the edge and sprawled on the ground to catch his breath. The gale at the top was strong enough to blow a man over. When Egner didn't show, Phillips peered down.

"Come on, Boats!" he yelled.

"I can't," wheezed Egner.

"Yes, you can. I made it, and so can you."

Flat on his stomach, Phillips stretched his arm down, clamped a hand around Egner's wrist and hauled him, inch by tortuous inch, up the steep incline until he was able to grab the back of his jacket and heave him over the edge.

After a quick breather, Phillips looked around. "Hey," he said, pointing down the gully, "there's a shed down there."

A shed meant that there must be people nearby. He and Egner slid to the bottom, Phillips close behind Egner as they neared the shed. Inside, lying in a state of exhaustion in the mess of hay, were the men who had followed Bergeron up the cliff. Petterson was one of them. Bergeron had gone for help.

Phillips and Egner decided to keep walking—before they froze to death.

CHAPTER 4
ST. LAWRENCE

The gale pushed Ena through the door and banged it shut behind her. She paused on the mat, flicking ice pellets from her hair. The place was unusually quiet. None of the staff were about.

"Ena, come here." Mr. Hollett, phone receiver in hand, stood in the doorway of his office.

No pleasantries this morning. His face was grim, his tone, too. She crossed the floor in double time and followed him into his office. What had she done? She was still learning the finer points of her position at Hollett Sons & Co. Ltd.—though her goofs were steadily decreasing. Mr. Hollett ran a finger down a list of phone numbers taped to his desk. Pausing under one, he looked up at her.

"There's an American warship ashore. At Chambers Cove."

Ena squawked, echoing his words—trying to make this astounding information register in her mind. A warship? Ashore? In Chambers Cove? Ena thought of the cars she'd seen rushing toward Iron Springs. Chambers Cove was a rare sunny summer's day, berry-picking kind of place. Heaven forbid that anyone venture anywhere near there in winter.

Mr. Hollett gave her no time to process the horror of it. "The staff are gone to Iron Springs to see what they can do. You're to keep the store open. There'll be a truck along to pick up supplies."

Nodding, Ena hung her coat and pulled up the sleeves of her sweater. She called after Mr. Hollett as he headed for the door, "Is there anything else?"

"Clear the shelves first. Then the stockroom. Give them whatever they ask for."

Ena hurried down to the basement to start packing boxes.

▼▲▼

Shoulder to the gale, Gus sprinted along the path. The going, rough enough through brush, was even rougher when he broke out into open country.

A stretch of grassland in summer, this morning it was sheeted in ice that whipped his feet from under him. To his left, the storm-ridden seas, thundering against the shore, were deafening. Gus couldn't imagine being out there on a ship. The scraggy trail ahead, blown in here and there, veered away from the coast and wound up over the hill. He pulled his wool cap farther down over his ears and forehead.

Almost halfway, he met up with Rennie Slaney and Rube Turpin with two sailors stumbling and weaving alongside them.[52] They looked like they'd been dumped in a barrel of tar and had fared badly. Gus could barely tear his eyes from them. They were barely conscious. The two bosses from Iron Springs were heading back to the mine for more help. Gus told Rennie that Theo was on his way too. Driven by the frightful state of the sailors, he sped along, slipping and sliding as he ran, until he reached the brook, running full and wild.

Crossing the bridge, he noted smears of oil on the rickety railing. He skated across it, a bundle of jumpy nerves and strangled breaths, and reached the hay tilt. Four men were crammed inside, black with fuel oil and shivering under some hay. The sailors said that they were all right and urged him to hurry on to help the men on the beach and on the ship. "Walk to the mine," Gus told them. "It's only half an hour from here." Three managed to haul themselves upright; the last man couldn't pluck up the energy to move.

---

52   Harry (Boats) Egner and Lanier Phillips.

Knowing that more help was on the way, Gus continued up the incline toward the rim of the cove. Ice glazed the hummocks and pockets of crusty snow camouflaged the hollows. He fell, lost the rope, and had to slide back for it. He swore a few choice words on his way down and on the way back up when again he almost lost his footing.

He kept looking back.

Hoping that the sailors in the tilt had started out for Iron Springs.

▼▲▼

Clara, with an armful of blankets and a flour bag of clothes belonging to Patrick, and Aunt Mary, who was hugging a boiler of soup, climbed into the back of the stake body mine truck. Along the way, they picked up more women walking toward the wreckage; most toted supplies. She was surprised to see horses and sleighs already on the way as well as a young fellow with a dog sled piled high with quilts. By the time they turned up the road to Iron Springs, the back of the truck was crowded with women, blankets, pots and pans (both empty and full), tea kettles, and anything else they could carry.

The old truck eased over and around the potholes, negotiating the rough 3-mile stretch to the mine site. Clara prayed that the sailors would survive. That the town's men could get to them. She'd spent many a grand fall day on the barrens above Chambers Cove picking cranberries and partridgeberries. But on a day like this?

The very thought petrified her.

▼▲▼

Ena hustled back and forth from shelves to stockroom to counter, gathering everything in the store that could be useful.

She packed tea, crackers, cans of soup, milk, and whatever else she guessed might come in handy into boxes and bags. Blankets, towels, ear caps, mitts and gloves, wool socks, and even the few jackets in stock, she piled on the counter. The war coming so close to home was a shock. She was well aware that Newfoundland, a colony of Great Britain, was considered to be at war. Her boyfriend, Robert, had joined the Royal Canadian Air Force and was away training on the mainland before being shipped overseas. She missed him, slept with his letters under her pillow, and couldn't bear the thought of him going off to fight.

For the last two years there had been a military presence in St. Lawrence. The Newfoundland Regiment had built barracks near Clarke's Pond. She thought of Robert every time she saw them do their drills and march through town. There was also a small group of Royal Canadian Engineers. Thinking how little there was for them to do when they were off duty, Ena had formed a voluntary service club among the young people to entertain them. Every week a different group hosted a social: dances, singalongs, and games in the parish hall, ending with a tasty lunch. The leftovers were sent back to the barracks, where rations were reported to be awful, with the soldiers.

As well, the whole coast was under blackout—the Atlantic was infested with German subs. Since the coastal boat was the only means of travel along the coast, last summer her parents hadn't allowed her to visit her cousins in St. John's. Ena had been ticked off at that. Still, except for missing Robert, her life had not been overly affected by the war. There was no conscription, so her brothers were all home and working. Her father was a businessman; she didn't want for anything. Up to now, the biggest inconvenience was that nylons were hard to come by; the girls had to resort to wearing cotton stockings. Sugar, too, was in short supply—and Ena did like a generous spoonful of sugar in her tea. This morning though, everything had changed.

How could she help?

▼▲▼

Gus closed in on the last few feet. To the west, Pinnacle Head reared up some 300 feet.

Its base was a mass of raging white water. Directly ahead, Tom Beck looked down on the cove. Gus joined him, shielding his face from the vicious gale flinging pelletized sleet and splatters of oil 50 feet up the cliff. Squinting against the assault, he looked down. A few hundred yards offshore lay the huge destroyer. She was keeled over at a 45-degree angle, her massive hull manacled by a crib of rocks. A slew of sailors clung to safety lines at her railing. He didn't know what he had expected, but not this. Stunned, he had no words, no thoughts.

Slowly, he began to register the sight. The cove was black as death. Cliffs, shingle, and seas--all shrouded in a pall of oil and wreckage. Waves climbed halfway up the cliffs and smashed back down. Sailors attempting to swim ashore dropped into the troughs and popped back up (after what seemed to Gus like an eternity) striking out for the spinning boats again, only to be flung off every time. The sea was dotted with bodies and debris. Sailors clung to anything that floated: wreckage, gummed-up life rafts that were ripped out of their hands on 5-foot waves. Tom and Gus stared, mesmerized.

Moving back from the edge, Tom filled Gus in. He, Mick Turpin, and Syl Edwards had been warming up by the fire after they'd loaded an ore truck for transport to the mill when Mick saw a young fellow coming up over the marsh calling for help. Stumbling and falling around, he was. Mick ran to him; he said he'd come from the cove. He was on a destroyer; they'd run ashore. Mick brought the sailor to the mine house to warm him up. In the mess room, they sat him by the stove and asked him to repeat his story. Albert Grimes and Robert Turpin were there. Rennie came out of his office too. But the young fellow was ansty, wanting to get help for his shipmates.

Mick grabbed a coil of rope and Tom, Mick, and Syl cut straight across the hills for the cove, with the young fellow following. With no path, the going was rough, but it was faster, and they reached the gully and tilt in a half-hour.

"I saw the men in the tilt," Gus said. "I tried to get them to go on."

Tom nodded. "They're not in great shape to walk, but someone will pick them up shortly."

Gus noticed a handline lying on the ground.

"The young fellow must have left it here for his shipmates," Tom said.

The light line looped a chunk of ice and trailed down the incline.

▼▲▼

The truck pulled up in front of the mess house.

The new building had been constructed less than a year before. It had a dry room, with an actual toilet, where the miners could change before and after their shifts, and a separate lunchroom, complete with stove and running water. In no time, the women had turned it into a makeshift hospital. Clara was glad to see Nurse Reddy and District Nurse Sadie Ash, both of whom she knew. They were posted at nursing stations along the coast and travelled back and forth on the SS *Kyle*, the coastal boat. As a midwife, Clara worked in consultation with both nurses when there were medical complications with the health of a mother and baby.

"Thank God you're here," Clara told the nurses.

Clara had seen tar before. She'd watched her father tar the roof of their house. But to see a man drenched in tar—so thick, so heavy he was only recognizable as a human being by his white teeth—shook her to the depths of her soul. Laid out on the lunch table, the sight of him brought her to tears.

Nurse Reddy, still wearing her coat, worked at cutting through the inert man's clothes. "Crude oil," she said tersely, and called for more tables.

At the end of the room, Nurse Ash unpacked bandages, towels, syringes, and thermometers. "The *Kyle* docked last night to wait out the storm," she said. "Captain Connors tried to get near to help this morning, but with the seas and the gale, it wasn't possible."

At first, Clara didn't see a second sailor curled up in a ball in front of the stove. Until he moaned. His whole body heaved in violent shakes. She grabbed a towel and went to him. Margaret O'Flaherty, a passenger from the *Kyle*, joined her. The two women lifted the helpless sailor onto a table. Plastered in oil, ears stogged, eyelashes glued shut, limbs frozen and semi-conscious, the fellow was in no shape to doctor himself. Clara grabbed towels, a blanket, and scissors from the supply table. Nurse Reddy began to cut off his clothes. Clara retrieved Pat's sweater and dungarees from the pile of clothes. They were going to need a lot more—of everything—once the others started arriving. "We need wash tubs, towels, rags, more quilts and blankets, more clothes, underwear too, and food and scissors and knives."

"On the way," someone told her.

Minutes later, the door blew open on a clump of battered, tarry sailors.

Drained of their last dregs of energy, they collapsed on the floor.

"More tables," roared Clara.

With nothing left in the store, Ena locked up.

All around the harbour, mine trucks were picking up supplies and anyone who could help. She'd get her toboggan, a 10-seater, collect canned food and clothes, and deliver it to the trucks. Delighted with the idea, she telephoned Julia and Ethel. Within the hour, the girls were traipsing up and down lanes, through gardens, and along the roads. Word of the disaster had spread, and it seemed that everyone was out on their stoops and porches. Uncle Dick Loder, at the end of his laneway, waved down a mine truck every now and then for the latest information.

Mrs. Edwards[53] of the Women's Patriotic Association led them into her front room. It was a veritable wool store—every surface and the blanket spread on the floor piled high with mitts, gloves, sweaters, scarves, helmets, and socks—all sizes, all colours and styles. Ena had seen her mother and Gran knitting for the war effort but had no idea how much the women of St. Lawrence had actually done. The girls helped Mrs. Edwards stuff pillowcases and flour bags with the knitting—a full bale,[54] she told them. Two hundred items or more. Ena was flabbergasted. The girls flagged down a mine truck. By the time they added their parcels of food and clothing, the truck was full. The women also asked for wash tubs, more towels, blankets, and underwear, the driver told them.

Ena knew just where to go. Mrs. Slaney had a houseful of men: her husband, his elderly father, and three teenage boys. Sure enough, the clothesline over the stove was lined off with long johns. She snapped them off and handed them to the girls. "If it wasn't for the sleet," she said with a laugh, "they'd all be frozen stiff on the line." She emptied the water from her galvanized wash tub and ran after them with that too.

The girls had a grand laugh on their way out the door, long johns streeling along behind them on the canvas floor.

▼▲▼

Gus grabbed the line and tied it around his waist.

"Your father will have my hide for this," Tom said as he dug in his

---

53   I was unable to locate the identity of the head of the Women's Patriotic Association. Edwards is a common surname.
54   Edwards, *St. Lawrence and Me*, 42.

heels and payed out the rope, easing Gus over the edge of the cliff.

Gus worked his way down the cliff face to the beach. The wind funnelling into the cove somewhat cushioned his descent. The overhang kept him from seeing the strip of shingle until he sank to the top of his rubber boots in black sludge. The tide was still rising, leaving only about 6 feet of beach at the base of the cliff. A heavy scum of stinking fuel stretched out about 25 feet from shore. The pungent smell took his breath. Turned his stomach. He covered his mouth and nose; it didn't help. But at least the crude calmed the cove. He gawked at the wreckage and oil and sailors thrashing in the surf. God knows how many were being tossed about in the flotsam; many of them were already dead, he feared. Screwing up his eyes to better penetrate the weather, he couldn't distinguish the lumps of men from the lumps of wreckage. Propelled by the wind, some drifted toward the beach.

At the edge of the shingle, Mick and Syl hauled sailors ashore. Flailing about, slathered in cold, thick crude and fighting the overpowering suck of wind and waves, the sailors struggled to crawl to their knees.

Farther up the beach, Pop dragged around two sorry-looking sailors, one under each arm. An officer, according to the insignia Gus noticed on his jacket, was doing the same with another survivor. The poor sailor seemed to Gus more dead than alive.

Just offshore, the wreck listed. Heavy seas smashed down on the men on board and barrelled on, washing one man overboard before his eyes. A few minutes later, while Gus was still getting his bearings, Theo arrived on the shingle and headed straight for the officer and a young seaman who was signalling the ship that help was on the way. Gus clomped along behind his brother. Mick and Syl, with no one to haul ashore at the moment, joined them. The officer, who said his name was Loughridge, said how grateful they were for the rescue party's help. He informed them that about 24 men had come ashore on life rafts and explained how they'd tried to get the life rafts back to the ship, but the lifeline had snagged and they'd had to cut it.

Gus had been keeping out of his father's way in case he got an earful about being down on the shingle, but he could no longer ignore Pop's beckoning to him. He tramped across the shingle, bracing himself for a telling-off. When he got there, Pop said, "Make yourself useful." He adjusted his hold on his charges and ordered Gus to get a fire going. "We have to keep them moving until we can send them up ... and stay back from the water."

Gus looked around. Not much to burn. He scoured the rocks, turning up a scattered stick of driftwood, blankets, and a sodden, oily life jacket. Nothing would catch. His father sent someone to the top with orders to send a horse and sleigh to the mine for a can of kerosene. While he waited, Gus, too shocked to feel anything—least of all the cold—lumbered over the tarry rocks dragging survivors with him. None of them were dressed for the conditions. Missing shoes. Some wore only pants, having jumped from their bunks when they hit. All carried 50 pounds or more of congealed oil.

Gus kept a close eye on Theo, as did his father. Pop tore off across the shingle, shaking a fist in alarm, when his brother and Syl, roped around the waist and tethered to men on shore, waded into the sludge heading for the ricocheting raft caught not far offshore. Seas rolled over their shoulders. They reached the raft, tugged and tugged, but it was caught hard. They trudged back to the beach, roaming the shoreline. Gus saw Pop have a word with Theo—or a word or two *at* Theo was more like it.

Outside the wreck, a coastal boat manoeuvred closer and closer. One of the miners said that it was the *Kyle*, with Captain Connors. Gus watched, heart in his mouth. Connors nudged the ship to within a few hundred yards of the cove, but could come no farther. He backed off.

More miners were at the beach now. A line of about 30, Mick and his brother Pius among them, stood up to their chests in crude and slush and wreckage. With seas breaking hard over their shoulders, they snagged sailors by the necks of their life jackets—the only place they could latch on—and passed them along in a human chain to shore. Gus's legs jellied with relief every time a sailor made it. Many drifted out to sea; many more were thrown onto the rocks or caught by vicious waves and hurled against the cliffs. Only a few were lucky enough to reach the outstretched arms of a waiting rescuer.

It looked like half the town had gathered at the clifftop, peering down and dropping blankets. Finally, a can of kerosene was lowered down. Pop sprinkled a few of the blankets with gas and told Gus to light it. With the tide at its peak, the water ran right up to the little fire. Gus figured it was a miracle that it had caught. There was more smoke than flame, but the men gravitated to the paltry bit of heat, except for a young sailor, slathered in fuel oil, who lay curled up on the shingle. Pop told him to get the fellow up and keep him moving until they could get him up to the top. Gus knelt over him.[55]

"Hey, buddy, let me help you to the fire." He hoisted the sailor to his feet, as gentle as he could. "What's your name?"

"Bill ... Bill Butterworth."

Gus walked him around the fire. Tried to keep him talking. "Where're you from?"

No response. His knees buckled; all his weight leaned on Gus. But Gus was determined to keep him alert.

"How old are you?"

Gus draped his own old, sheepskin work jacket around the young fellow's shoulders while he searched the shore to find something to throw on the dwindling fire. He returned as fast as he could, but Butterworth had fallen to the shingle where Gus had left him, the water already lapping at his feet, his face turned into the collar of Gus's jacket.

---

55   MacIntyre, *The Wake*, 193.

The mine house was blessed with hot water, but the chill had gone deep inside the poor souls.

Clara gently wiped gobs of oil from the eyes and ears of the raving sailor on the table. The poor fellow had a bad case of the shakes. She called across the room. "We need hot water bottles; they're perishing here on the table."

"We're lighting fires outside and heating rocks" was the response.

Shortly after, another truck arrived with a group of boys carting armfuls of quilts, washtubs, towels, rags, and more soup. Past their ankles in sludge, the women tackled the sailors' clothing with scissors, knives, and bare hands. Their clothes were as stiff as a board and heavy with congealed crude. The men from town lined the cast iron stove, which was roaring full blast, with pots of soups and kettles that soon bubbled with tea and coffee. They hauled in tubs of heated rocks and bricks, which the women then wrapped in towels and packed around the chilled sailors. They handled the sailors as tenderly as they would their own children.

With more survivors arriving, the room, wall-to-wall with tables and tubs, was loud with the racket of sailors coughing up tarry oil and the shouts and moans of others suffering the pain of frozen limbs coming back to life. Even after hot scrubs, they were still seized with tremors and shaking as if palsied, afflicted by a chill squeezing their life force and causing their blood to run sluggish and cold through watery blue veins. The few who had revived enough to stand and walk were moved over to the dry room to wait for transportation to a home in St. Lawrence.

Clara, eyes tearing from the fumes and the sights, called for more hot rocks.

History was Ena's favourite subject in school.

All morning long, as she and her friends collected clothing and food, she stewed.

History, real history, was happening right here. Today. And she was unable to witness it. She desperately wanted to go to Chambers Cove with the Brownie camera she'd received for Christmas, but she didn't dare.

Her brother Howard was the assistant manager of the St. Lawrence Corporation, an American mining company. She wanted to capture local miners coming to the rescue of the American sailors. Her ideas often caused her straitlaced brother to bristle. She knew just what he would think of her going to the cove, surrounded by death and dying. To have his sister show up with a camera to take pictures of the tragedy—he'd faint! And she would be in big trouble.

Still, she couldn't let it go.

▼▲▼

The number of sailors at the ship's railing steadily dwindled. Gus couldn't tear his eyes away.

Word came down that Levi Molloy, Rennie Slaney, and Arch Slaney were trying to find a way to secure a line to the ship in order to ferry the crew ashore on a breeches buoy. They spliced together ropes from the *Kyle*, to run from one end of the cove across to Pinnacle Head at the other end, which they planned to drop down over the ship. Gus kept a squinty eye on the clifftop. The rope, dangling over the edge, became hooked by the breeze like a thread on an updraft, and was whipped inland every time they tried to launch it.

Shortly after, a Navy plane circled overhead, passing as low as she dared. There's nowhere to land here, Gus thought. The sight may have given the sailors hope, but the Newfoundlanders knew that if Connors hadn't been able to do anything, no one could. Not even the US Navy. Not by air. Not by sea.

Sailors drifted ashore in groups of twos and threes. The rescuers in the surf—Gus's brother among them—braced themselves to stay upright against a steady barrage of breakers. The tide had reached its peak and was finally falling. The seas were no calmer though. The gale had shifted to the west and was blowing directly into the cove, pushing 40-foot waves ahead of it.

Other miners prepared to bring survivors up the cliff: tie a rope around the fellow and have the men on the rim hoist him to the top. It seemed simple enough. The ride up, however, proved brutal. And took forever. Neil Tarrant, who was on a separate rope guiding the sailors away from icy humps and sharp stabs of rock, reported that the men were enduring a battering on the way up—cuts on their faces and hands, and heads bruised by the time they got past the overhang. Spent from exhaustion and exposure, they didn't have the reserves to help themselves. The miners decided to use the other side of the craggy cliff jutting out to the east. From there, the rescuers could see below and monitor the sailors' progress up the ravine.

Gus, walking a sailor around the puny fire, watched. Abe Pike hoisted a man—who was packing an extra 50 pounds of crude—over his shoulder, took him past the outcrop and down the other side into the next little cove, about 15 feet away, where both were pulled to the top. Back and forth he went. Pike worked like a Trojan, Pop said later. Mick Turpin did too. George Carr was another, as were Greg Edwards and Leo Loder. They carried the men across the shingle on their backs and put the strap around them both to get them up. At the top, eight or nine men hauled on the line to bring up the combined weight of two men.

Many locals waited at the top, ready to come below to assist when there was room on the shingle. Others stood by to help survivors to the hay tilt, where horses and sleighs waited, ready to take them to Iron Springs.

The *Truxtun* continued to take a severe pounding, the forward part falling more and more over on her side, her stern already separated; the bridge and four funnels had gone under. Waves surged the length of the ship. Shifting winds lacerated what remained of the deck, while violent seas mounted the hull and clobbered men on the safety lines. The after part had broken off completely, and each huge wave pushed the stern farther away.[56] The men at the railing still refused to jump. Gus couldn't blame them, not with the carnage all around them.

Lionel Saint, a bottle of St. Pierre rum tucked under his arm, and his son-in-law, Ferdinand Giovannini, arrived on the shingle. Lionel passed the bottle around to sailors circling the fire. One fellow yelped in pain when the liquor cut into a gash on his lip. When the bottle was empty, Lionel and his son-in-law helped to keep the survivors on their feet.

Gus trucked across the beach after his brother. A sailor reported to Loughridge that the ship was signalling. Theo asked what they were saying.

"Boats ... they want boats," he replied.

Miners and survivors chimed in. "Impossible in these seas." "Jump and swim with the waves." "No other way ..."

On Loughridge's orders, Parkerson, knee deep in crude, swung his arms, messaging the ship.

From the railing, the flags wigwagged back and forth—an intermittent signal broken by sleet and spume. *Boats. Send boats.*

"It's not possible to get a boat out to the ship," Theo told Loughridge. "Not while the seas are like this."

Loughridge agreed.

"Maybe they can't cipher the signals," Theo suggested.

That made sense to Gus. With the signalman as black and sludged up as the oily shingle he stood on, and under the curtain of heavy skies, they likely couldn't see. Theo grabbed a white woollen blanket and

---

56   Brown, *Standing into Danger*, 195.

draped it over a slate grey crude-spattered rock protruding from the side of the cliff. It stuck to the tarry oil, suctioned to the cliff by the gale blasting into the cove. "Go stand in front of it," he instructed Parkerson. "Tell them to swim. Tell them it's the only way."

Parkerson worked his way along the ledge. He planted himself in front of the blanket and swung his arms. The miners cautioned him: "Warn them to stay outside the point—by 30 feet at least." The wind would take them around it and in toward the beach.

Over and over, the *Truxtun*'s Signalman Brom waved his flags: *Boats.*

Over and over, onshore Parkerson signalled back: *Jump.*

With ebbtide, the water receded, leaving a foot-deep overlay of gelled crude underfoot in the landwash. And more lifeless bodies. Waiting for more sailors to come ashore, the men scoured the shingle, carefully bearing bodies and parts of bodies to the base of the cliff for burial later. Gus cringed. Cried. Busied himself with tending to the fire and the half-dead seamen circling it.

At the far end of the shingle, miners were still bringing survivors up the cliff. Those on the beach were busy with ailing survivors or with trying to get the men at the railing to slide off and swim. Someone came back down and reported that the word at the top was that a fair-sized patch of oil and junk was drifting along the coast toward Chambers Cove. Lionel went above to check it out.

For over two hours, Parkerson stood on the exposed ledge, signalling directions to his partner on the listing port wing: *Jump. Swim to the mouth of the cove.*

Then the ship's mast snapped. The forward section fractured again, breaking the destroyer into three pieces. Heavy seas drove between. A huge wave took upward of 30 men. Gus buckled at the knees, blindsided by the sight. The suddenness. The certainty. Then he saw heads bobbing in the water. Those who struck out for the nearest shoreline had no chance. They met instant death against the cliff. Another sea took 20 more. Only a few tried to swim. The others flailed about in the waves—until they too were bashed against the cliffs.

Theo, ignoring Pop's consternation, made his way over the slick boulders and around the point where he waved the sailors offshore, away from the razor-sharp rocks. The seas pummelled the *Truxtun*. Another mammoth wave buried the ship and the few men on the forecastle. When it retreated, only six seamen could be seen slumped over the rail. The *Truxtun*'s signalman was not one of them.

The Newfoundlanders helped Parkerson down from his post and across the shingle. Gus, back to rooting among the rocks for something to burn, couldn't help staring, in awe of the young signalman. Throughout the morning, he had turned down a half-dozen chances to go up with the others. He told the rescuers that someone had to maintain contact with the ship. He figured that he was the best man to do it. Parkerson shuffled around the fire until he slumped on the strand, afflicted by a heart-wrenching case of the shakes. The miners tucked blankets around him. Rubbed his frozen limbs. He died not long after, calling "Mother."

The men dragged an American flag from the muck, wiped it off as best they could, and covered Parkerson with it.

▼▲▼

Clara was about to go for clean water.

"I used up three cloths just wiping the oil out of his hair," Violet said. "Look, Clara, have you ever seen such a lovely head of curls?"

Clara glanced at the semi-conscious sailor twitching in discomfort on the table and sent up a silent prayer for him. When she got back, Violet was still going on about the awful state he was in. Tackling his ears and neck, Violet rubbed and rubbed. All the while taking care to be gentle on his skin. Poor soul. He had endured enough.

"My sweet Lord, it's right in his pores," she said with a heavy sigh, when he wasn't coming clean like the others.

The sailor stirred. His eyes flickered open briefly and he stammered, "Ma'am, that's the colour of my skin."

Violet, Clara, and the other women laughed.

Violet patted his cheek. "Don't you worry, my dear, we'll get it off."

The sailor's eyes closed.

As the morning wore on, the number of arriving survivors dwindled. Cleaned up and conscious, they were fed, dressed in whatever the women could lay a hand on, and trucked off to the homes of many of the same people who had brought them back to life.

Clara suggested to Mary and Pauline that they go to the cove in case there were more survivors. Halfway, they met Father Thorne. As the parish priest, he'd been on the clifftop all day ministering to the survivors. Father's cassock, soaking wet, filthy, and slathered in stinking crude, stuck to his legs, making walking a trial—the cruddy frozen hem swaying like a crooked hoop.

"Father, are there any more survivors?" Clara asked.

"Just one," Father Thorne replied. "He came ashore hand over hand on the dory line. They're waiting for a sleigh to bring him in."

"Let's go check," Clara urged Mary and Pauline.[57]

---

57   Mary (Isaac) and Pauline Loder. Turpin, telephone conversation with author, October 8, 2020; and Cyril Tarrant (Clara's son), email messages to author, September and October 2020.

CHAPTER 5
USS *POLLUX*

Lieutenant Junior Grade William C. Grindley, navigator aboard the *Pollux*, was an experienced seaman. This was not his first time navigating these seas.

Called up from the Merchant Navy to active duty in the US Navy in 1940, after the National Defense Act was passed in Congress, Grindley, third in command, oversaw the navigational team and the communications department. In addition, he was senior watch officer, tasked with training deck watch officers aspiring to the rank of watch officers. He was also charged with overseeing the operations of the library, ship's stores, laundry, barbershop, cobbler shop, tailor shop, and the soda fountain. Grindley was a busy man.[58] But this morning, he was all navigator.

From the minute he'd stepped on the bridge at 0345 hours, the day had been trying, and only worsened as the hours ticked by. Though the horizon was hazy, at 0620 hours he managed to grab three star sights before clouds closed in again. Better than nothing. At 1000 hours and again at 1100 hours, he finally caught sun lines. All lined up with their dead-reckoning plot, which enabled him to lay down a new course that would take them up the middle of Placentia Bay. Course 47 degrees true, steering course 55 degrees true, favoured the east side of Placentia Bay and allowed for leeway to make the 47 degrees course good.

Commander Hugh Turney, on the bridge since 0700 hours, agreed. "It's a good, safe course."

---

58   Brown, *Standing into Danger*, 20.

Grindley was familiar with the sailing directive for Newfoundland that cautioned mariners about a westerly set from the arctic current. In the event of a westerly set, the RDF bearings on Gallantry Head lighthouse (on St. Pierre Island) and Latine Point lighthouse (on the northwest corner of Argentia Peninsula) would help them make a good landfall.[59] Considering that all morning strengthening winds backed from the north, Grindley suggested to Turney, "Maybe even more leeway, sir?"

Turney shook his head. "No, the course is sound." He ordered a signal sent to the *Wilkes* about changing course to 55 degrees at noon.

However, the flagship overruled both Grindley and Turney. The *Wilkes* flashed a message that there would be no course change until 2000 hours. A 1200-hour change of course would have increased the angle from land on the west side of Placentia Bay—the longer the run, the greater the angle.[60] The delay until 2000 hours would close that angle, taking them possibly as much as 5 to 8 miles off course and closer to land.

On this run, the *Wilkes* called the shots. She bombarded them with endless bulletins and dispatches. Earlier in the day, after they'd rounded Cape Sable, Nova Scotia, a succession of pointed messages from the *Wilkes* detailed their speed and position. This last order to change course so late in the day made both Grindley and Turney uneasy.

"Where are we?" Turney asked, irritation evident.

Grindley replied, "I managed to get a sun sight at 1220 hours, but due to the foggy horizon it's an approximation."

At 1400 hours, Grindley fixed a more reliable sun sight, assuring him that they were approaching Artimon Bank, located about 150 miles east of Cape Breton Island. He noted slush ice drifting south across the *Pollux*'s bow: a reliable indicator that the set of the current was still

---

59   Brown, *Standing into Danger*, 37.
60   Brown, *Standing into Danger*, 37, 38.

away from land; he was content with that. From there, he plotted their 1600-hour position toward St. Pierre Bank. Once on the fishing bank, they would know with certainty their location.

The weather had been rotten since they formed convoy and steamed out of Casco Bay, Maine, two days ago. All afternoon sleet had pelted the ship, icing the decks. Later, snow and hail added to the mix. The Force 5 wind breezed up steadily, provoking a fury of a blizzard. Tied to Zigzag Plan 26, Grindley was frustrated. He was a man who spoke his mind, and he could no longer hold back.

"Sir," Grindley blurted, "with so many broad changes of course, adhering to Plan 26 makes it impossible to correct the leeway." Tapping his pencil on the chart table, he drew a breath before continuing. "I'm not able to compensate for the wind and waves hitting the starboard beam." He paused. "I recommend we stop zigzagging."

Turney faced Grindley, his face and his stance rigid, his reply curt: "Commander Webb, the senior officer of this convoy, will determine what action, if any, is required. No orders have been received from the *Wilkes*. Until an order is given, we will continue to zigzag."

Grindley understood. The *Pollux* was Turney's first command. He was not about to be reprimanded again by the *Wilkes* and shown up in front of his crew. The frustration between the two men continued to grow through the long, wearing evening.

Northern skies brought darkness fast. At 1900 hours, visibility was only 700 yards.[61] "Reduce speed," Grindley prodded. He had done so on previous runs when approaching Placentia Bay in heavy seas and weather.

Turney stalled, rubbing his forehead; he was not sure. Then, reconsidering, he penciled a message to the *Wilkes: Poor visibility. Suggest we reduce speed to 8 knots.* He made to hand the note to the quartermaster to transmit, then pulled back, and ripped it to

---

61   Brown, *Standing into Danger*, 41.

pieces. "Better not," he said. "The *Wilkes* seems to be making all the suggestions."[62]

Grindley paced to hide his fury. With 12 years' experience navigating the storm-ridden, foggy, western North Atlantic, he knew these waters. He had sailed this coastline, navigated the tricky currents. After he logged their approach to St. Pierre Bank, he greeted Lieutenant Schmidt, who had arrived for the 2000-hour watch, informed him that they were on the approach to St. Pierre Bank, and added that he had not yet nailed down their exact position. Schmidt left for the obligatory turn outside to get his night vision.

Grindley felt the question of their position was so serious as to conceivably be disastrous. Alone in the chart room with Turney, he determined to make a case for using the fathometer. He straightened up, crossed his arms, and stated, "Sir, I know we're under orders not to use the fathometer, that submarines are adept at picking up the ship's radiation. But, as navigator, I feel that in these adverse conditions tonight it's necessary." He paused. "It's our only chance to fix position before we drop off the northern edge of the bank." Before Turney could object, he added, "The radiation isn't much, 5 miles maybe, if that."

Commander Turney, visibly annoyed, pursed his lips. They were under strict orders from the flagship not to use the fathometer. The directive was reasonable, necessary. Grindley understood that his superior was under pressure. The tension in the room was palpable, radiating from them both.

Finally, with barely a nod, Turney relented. "Run the fathometer," Turney ordered the sound operator. "And keep it running." Then he left to grab an hour's shut-eye on his cabin transom, next to the chart house.

Both men were exhausted. Grindley had been on the bridge for 20 hours, Turney for 17. However, sleep was not an option for Grindley. He stared at their track, stewing over each sounding the operator

---

62   Brown, *Standing into Danger*, 41.

delivered, knowing that once they dropped off the north edge of St. Pierre Bank, the uncertainty of their position increased. RDF bearings were already diminishing, the null area widening as they steamed north and away from the sending stations.[63] The *Pollux*'s plotted course up the west side of Placentia Bay would take them about 20 miles off land, and off Cape St. Mary's, on the eastern side, by approximately 25 miles. However, navigation from St. Pierre Bank to Placentia Bay (with speed, depth, uniform sea bottom, and shoaling close to shore all factors in play) was as much about experience and gut feeling as it was about maps and calculations.

The next watch clocked in shortly before 2400 hours. The ship rolled; wild seas cascaded across her deck, thickening the layers of ice. The guns, too, were iced up. Back in the chart house, Turney ordered the gun crews inside. "But stay alert," he warned.

According to the soundings, they were slightly north of their track—not by much, but enough that Grindley anxiously awaited each new fathometer reading. Between 0020 and 0030 hours, soundings indicated that the *Pollux* had crossed St. Pierre Bank an hour ahead of her plotted time at a narrower track and northward. The ship was on the other side of the gully cutting into the bank, 5 miles northwest of their base track; and they had been set 11 degrees to the northwest.[64]

Turney studied the plot Grindley had laid down. "There must be a small westerly current."

Grindley agreed, sort of. When it came to St. Pierre Bank, being off course was a given. Low visibility, no landmarks, no star sights, and frequent westerly currents made for a more or less normal run across the bank. However, the *rate* of drift tonight had Grindley's nerves twitching. Eleven degrees to the northwest while crossing the bank was bloody dangerous. They were rolling sideways as much as

63   Brown, *Standing into Danger*, 43.
64   Brown, *Standing into Danger*, 60.

steaming ahead. The *Pollux* was headed for the rocks. Grindley knew it. Unable to pin down their position, he pressed Turney, "Sir, we need to reverse course out of here. Fast!"

Turney would not hear of it.

Grindley tried a different tact. He suggested that they return to St. Pierre Bank until morning when they could see their approach to Placentia Bay. He informed Turney, "Sir, I've done it before when sailing to Argentia in stormy weather."

Turney would not hear of it. "Under Navy regulations, we follow the orders of the flagship. The *Wilkes* has radar, and they haven't signalled trouble."

Grindley was livid. He had seen radar. It was not all it was touted to be. With the coastline, the ship, and even the cursed antennas clamped in ice, it might pick up land at 2 miles, but not the 20 miles Turney was fixed on. Grindley realized that Turney was in a bind: his ship or his Navy career. Not much leeway there. Flouting orders was a tough prospect. Grindley's reputation was at stake too. Clamping his mouth shut before he pushed too far, he removed himself from the chart room to grab a coffee in the officer's wardroom.

He returned to find Turney pacing from charts to fathometer and back. To mollify Grindley, and to ease his own considerable concern, Turney agreed to change course 10 degrees right. Grindley wanted more.

"Sir," Grindley said, "10 degrees just adds leeway to the course we're steering now. We need at least 30 degrees!"

Turney would not budge. And on the zigzag, he would not yield at all. Orders. Near 0130 hours, he wrote a message to the flagship advising that the *Pollux* had changed base course 10 degrees to the right and ordered it sent by visual signal with the small blinker gun.

Ensign Robert Grayson reported back that the message had been sent, but no Roger had been received in return. Grayson logged the message but did not record the fact that the *Wilkes* had not responded.

Grindley, troubled, and angry, drew up a new zigzag plan for the helmsman to follow on the new course, 57 degrees true. The 10-degree shift was inadequate, negligible. With punishing winds and waves propelling them northwest toward land, they needed to set right 30 degrees or more.

They needed to stop the zigzag. Grindley could taste disaster.

▼▲▼

The crew of the *Pollux*—mostly from the New York area—and together since training—were a tight bunch, on and off duty.

Routinely, the *Pollux* sailed with a crew of 143 enlisted men and 16 officers. This run the *Pollux* also carried 16 passengers for the USS *Prairie* in Argentia and 58 new recruits who were shipping to Argentia for training, after which they'd be stationed on ships in the North Atlantic theatre.[65]

Before setting sail, Fireman 1st Class Lawrence Calemmo and his buddies had strolled down to the Brooklyn Navy Yard, where the *Pollux* was commissioned in May, 1941, for a look. There'd been robust swearing when she came into view. She was not the slick destroyer they had trained for. They'd sniggered at the fresh coat of grey paint. She was a tub. "A floating coffin," Calemmo had cracked. The feeling stayed with him.

Like it or not, Calemmo and his mates crewed aboard the *Pollux* from her commissioning day. He did his best to ensure their safety. As the ship's engineer, he was part of the lifeboat crew. He took no chances with the touchy diesel engines; he rigged his own heaters with four 100-watt bulbs tucked inside metal boxes. He installed them under the engine hoods and babied them with constant checks. If a U-boat scoped them, his lifeboats would be in prime condition.

---

65   Brown, *Standing into Danger*, 14.

At 0345 hours, Calemmo, already suited up, was on the crew for Number One Motor Whaleboat watch. With the severe weather, Turney had given them permission to shelter in the midship passageway. Stuffed into his foul weather gear, Calemmo pried open the heavy door, bracing himself. Winds geared up to gale force screamed through the rigging, slinging snow and sleet across the bow. The *Pollux* rode up a wall of black water, shivered atop, and sank into a stomach-turning trough before rearing to do it all over again. Calemmo hung on. He shot the dirty night an equally dirty scowl and dropped to his hands and knees.

Flattening to the deck, he hauled himself across to the whaleboat, wrestling the weather all the way. He slid over the icy gunwale and landed on his behind. The heater was still working, the light bulb glowing steadily in spite of the weather and seas. The diesel engine sputtered and chugged. Steady. Even. Calemmo grinned, feeling like a god. While the engine warmed up, he checked out the boat, chiselled some ice, and inspected the davit wires. Once the diesel was toasty and purring, he shut it down.

He looked over the whaleboat one more time and waved to the crew that he was making his way back—ready for a coffee.

Fireman 2nd Class Ernest L. Califano took a moment for his face to thaw. He blinked repeatedly and felt ice chips dislodge and slide down his cheeks.

He had just come off the 0000-to-0400-hour lifeboat watch. *Grateful* didn't do justice to how glad he was that it was over. His eyelashes felt as if they were individually encased in rime. Fingers useless duds, he shrugged out of his foul weather gear and left it in a heap at the end of the passageway. The lifeboat crew was there. His pal Calemmo called to him above the din. "Hey there, Ernie. Hang around for a coffee. I'll be right back."

"Sure," Califano hollered back. "Not like there's much chance of shut-eye on this bucket tonight."

The crew yakked while they warmed up. "Commander Turney and Grindley are at odds tonight," one fellow said, keeping his voice low.

True. During his watch, Califano had sensed something was up. As Grindley and Turney travelled back and forth to the chart room, they had all heard the mutterings. Felt the tension.

A mate responded, "Below, I heard one of the petty officers coming off duty say that the navigator was arguing with the captain his whole shift, but he would clam up as soon as anyone entered the chart room."

The seaman looked at his buddy. "You heard him too? Seems it was about our position."

His pal nodded. "And the zigzag."

A third said, "Grindley wanted to change course 30 degrees to the right. The captain nixed that and allowed Grindley only 10 degrees."

The boys all nodded. Aboard ship, rumours spread like lice and gathered legs with each telling. Califano listened but said nothing, not wishing to give more credence to the idle talk. He had been on watch on the starboard wing when Grayson and Signalman George Horner, a mate of Califano's, sent the message of the *Pollux*'s 0130-hour course change to 57 degrees. Califano was glad that it wasn't his job. Grayson and Horner seemed to take forever adjusting the searchlight into position. The seas were so rough that Grayson had to hold on to Horner so that he could flash the signal. On Horner's way inside, he'd said to Califano, "I hope the *Wilkes* got the message. I sent it twice to make sure." He added, "I got a blink back from her after each word, but no Roger at the end. Neither time."

Horner had looked worried about it. Califano could see why. The *Pollux* was under orders to follow the *Wilkes*, even in lousy weather like tonight. The zigzag made it hard enough to stay in convoy, but the idea of the *Wilkes* not receiving the message about their course change made Califano nervous. He refused to consider what could happen.

The talk turned to the usual aboard-ship chitchat: U-boats, icebergs, and a rumoured secret cargo of radar to be installed on destroyers in Argentia. A cargo of radar on board made them ripe pickings for a U-boat attack and was supposedly the reason for the convoy. The *Pollux* begrudged the escort. Her crew, a seasoned lot, cared diddly-squat about secret cargo. Their beef was with Navy stupidity; 2,000 to 3,000 yards on the *Pollux*'s starboard bow, the *Wilkes* ploughed through heavy seas. The same distance to port, the *Truxtun* plunged about. They were on a cursed collision course, the boys grumbled to each other. No one envied the officers on a night like this. They had good reason to be jumpy. Routinely, greenhorns went AWOL at the prospect of a North Atlantic run. Califano pulled out a cigarette and a box of matches. The boys on either side leaned in. Califano struck a match and lit all three.

"Hey," someone said, "that's three on a match."

Califano felt a sudden twist of dread in his innards. He recalled how a few years earlier he'd gone through the windshield of a Model A Ford when he and two pals lit up on a match.

"Shaddup and drink your coffee," one of the fellows snapped.

All hands knew that bad luck came in threes.

▼▲▼

From senior officers to junior seamen, the *Pollux*'s bridge hummed with activity. At 0345 hours, all watches were switched out and the oncoming teams briefed.

Grindley toiled over the charts, plotting the new course for the first leg of the 0400-to-0600-hour zigzag and studying the fathometer readings in efforts to nail down their position—as he had been doing since the ship's change of course to 57 degrees almost two hours ago.

Lieutenant Junior Grade George Bradley burst into the chart room ready to take over as OOD for the 0400-to-0800-hour deck watch. He rubbed his hands together to warm them and nodded in deference to Turney. "It's quite a night, sir," he said. Approaching the chart table, he asked Grindley, "What is our position, Lieutenant?"

Grindley straightened up, grimaced, and rubbed his lower back. He'd been leaning over that table all night. "Shortly after 0000 hours, we crossed St. Pierre Bank." He pointed his pencil to the area north of the gully on the northern side of the fishing bank. Moving the pencil along the track, he said, "And here's where we changed course to 57 degrees true."

Bradley nodded. "So 57 degrees true will take us south of Cloue Rock?" Cloue Rock was an important marker on the entrance to Placentia Bay.

"Correct."

Turney interjected, "At daybreak, you'll sight land to port."

Lieutenant Grade Bollinger, the junior OOD for the shift, stepped inside the chart room with a grin. "When the deck watch crew were taking up position on the port lookout of the flying bridge, one of the new recruits couldn't see in the driving sleet and ran smack into the lookout he was replacing!"

The officers chuckled. Turney said, "Those youngsters will get sea training tonight—more than they bargained for, I'm afraid."

Bollinger was glad that he could give Turney and Grindley a laugh. Both officers looked like they could use it. He'd never seen them look so worried. The old girl had weathered tough conditions on North Atlantic runs before. The watch officers and their crews settled into their routines for the next four hours. Bradley sent Bollinger to the flying deck, where the open area afforded unobstructed views of the fore, aft, and sides of the ship. With visibility practically nil at 600 yards, both men recognized the near futility of their task. "You'll also need to bolster the lookouts tonight. I'll take the starboard wing." Bradley headed off into the gale.

Turney passed an order for the forward gun watch—already saturated by hefty spray walloping the exposed gun mount and ricocheting back on them—to go inside the deckhouse for their safety.

Gindley kept pressing Turney. "Sir, it is imperative to cease the zigzag—until daylight, at least."

Turney, stony-faced, remained adamant.

Grindley strode back to the port wing. He squinted through the sleet. The gale had ratcheted up to a Force 8. The swells, too, had grown in size and in force: a sign that the water could be shallower than their plotted course indicated. Grindley might not be able to see land through the mess of weather, but he knew it was there. As sure as Uncle Sam. With every fibre of his being he felt an ominous, dark shadow looming over his shoulder. As they had been pushed off track by 5 miles between 2000 hours and 0023 hours, they were sure to be farther off course in the past four hours.[66] His ship was on a collision course for Lawn Head. They needed to get out of there—fast. Desperate, he approached Turney one final time.

At long last, Turney relented. Grindley's face registered his relief. He raced off to inform Bradley, but since he'd gone out on deck, he gave the order to Helmsman Meyers and sent a seaman on duty to inform Bradley.

On the same paper Turney had scribbled his first message to the *Wilkes*, he wrote: *I am coming to base course steady, speed 12 at 0430.* The *Pollux* was still sailing at 14 knots to make the required base speed of 12 knots, but as soon as the message was sent, they would reduce speed—as would the *Wilkes* and the *Truxtun*. Theoretically, all three ships would remain in formation.[67]

---

66   Brown, *Standing into Danger*, 96.
67   Brown, *Standing into Danger*, 97.

Neither Grindley nor Turney was aware that Horner had not received a Roger from the *Wilkes* to indicate receipt of the message of the *Pollux*'s course change to 57 degrees at 0130 hours. Grindley paused at the gyro repeater on the wing of the bridge to satisfy himself that they were steady on 57 degrees true. Next, he went to the wheelhouse, peered over Meyers's shoulder to double-check the course, and moved on to the starboard wing.

It was then that Quartermaster Thomas Turner picked up two searchlights in the distance: one trained down on the water, the other from an undetermined direction. He ran to the wheelhouse, yanked open the chart-house door, and shouted, "Bright lights ahead, sir."[68]

Bollinger, on the starboard wing of the flying bridge, had a clearer view. "Land! Dead ahead!" he roared.[69]

The lookout positions portside echoed his cry. In the glare of lights, Turney and Grindley dashed to the pilot house. A mass of land careened toward them.

"Hard right rudder,"[70] Turney barked, while ringing full astern on the engine-room telegraph.

Grindley burst out, "I knew it!"[71]

Bells, horns, and whistles shrilled, shrieked, and screeched, sounding the general alarm as the *Pollux*'s bow skewed hard right. She ploughed on, despite her engines grinding in reverse. She hit rock. Head-on. Officers and operators alike toppled about the tight space, like pins in a 10-pin bowling strike. The destroyer hove up, slammed down, hove up, and slammed down as might a mythic beast in grave distress. The time: 0417 hours.

Scrambling to his feet, Grindley made his way to the chart room to check their position. Lawn Head.

It had to be.

---

68   Brown, *Standing into Danger*, 98.
69   Brown, *Standing into Danger*, 98.
70   Brown, *Standing into Danger*, 98.
71   Brown, *Standing into Danger*, 98.

▼▲▼

Calemmo and the lifeboat crew were hunkered down in the starboard passageway.

On impact, they tumbled headlong—a knot of limbs, twisted and tangled as a can of spilled chain links. Foul weather gear sailed overhead like crazed seabirds. Projectile mugs ricocheted off the bulkhead and clipped the sides of their heads. Above the din of storm and gale, and the *Pollux*'s shudders and rumbles, the confined passageway echoed their roars:

"Torpedo!"

"Iceberg!"

"We're hit!"

Calemmo reclaimed his arms and legs and scrabbled to his knees bellowing, "No, we hit the *Truxtun!*" He intercepted a heavy weather jacket whipping by and shrugged it on, his motor launches top of mind. Were they still secure? And if they were, were they operational? Leaving his mates sorting themselves, he charged outside to the railing. For a second, maybe two or three, his mind would not—could not—register what his eyes were seeing, the shock so sudden he felt a stabbing pain right between his eyes. It was not a collision at sea. No gaping torpedo hole in the hull. No iceberg. Not even a trace of the *Truxtun*. Or the *Wilkes*.

They were up against rock, with more rearing up from the seas surrounding them.

▼▲▼

Califano picked up his gear and headed below, trying to stay upright.

For all his efforts, he was as successful as a drunk attempting to walk a straight line. He grabbed the door latch of his sleeping compartment and executed a masterful balancing act; he had no yen to enter headfirst. His insides lurching in tandem with the ship, he felt an unmistakable, whole-ship shiver.

And knew.

Instantly.

Deep in her belly, Califano felt the tremors through timber and steel. He catapulted through the door and spilled into the chaos of men being thrown smack to the deck. Fending off bunks ripped from their hinges, they fell about in the dark, crashing into one another until someone yelled for lights. The din of sirens, horns, bells, and whistles sent the men clamouring up the ladders to their emergency stations. Califano's damage control post was the port passage. Jostled about, he elbowed his way to the railing for a look. His eyes bulged big as taw marbles. Sure, they had yakked about a collision, knowing on a gut level it was a real possibility. But running into a cliff?

Not in his wildest imagination had Califano seen that coming.

▼▲▼

Grindley ordered Schmidt, "Send a message that we're aground."

Then he bolted outside to join Turney and his officers.

The *Pollux* was hard aground at the base of a steep headland. The port searchlight flickered over waves slung up the cliff by a ferocious gale, rebounding onto a sizable ledge projecting out from the bottom of the cliff, and then falling back full bore onto the *Pollux*'s foredeck. A menace of dark clouds skulked low over the crag's rim. No searchlight could penetrate that.

Quartermaster Turner sprinted toward Commander Turney. "Sir, the radioman received a message from the *Wilkes*. She's aground too."

Turney said nothing. Neither did Grindley. As far as Grindley was concerned, the *Wilkes* was on her own. The *Pollux* was their concern.

The force of 15 tons of iron and steel colliding with solid rock had breached the ship's hull forward of amidships—rammed it through. She listed to starboard, her bow bent and buried in sea water. Only the stern floated free at the mercy of a raging gale and wild surf. Still, the *Pollux* was afloat.

But not for long, Grindley gauged. The outlook for the ship was as bleak as the scarp rearing over them. With the weight of her broken bow and the seas savaging her hull, the supply ship would, before long, break in two. Turney ordered the engines stopped while they assessed their situation. Soundings were taken to determine the depth of the water. Bradley reported a strong undertow and a depth between 40 and 70 feet.

Grindley knew that Turney was concerned about the considerable hit the war effort would suffer if the *Pollux*, equipped with five cargo holds, were to sink. All would be lost: everyday necessities for the fleet, a considerable cache of money, aerial bombs, aircraft engines, radio and gun equipment, and the rumoured secret cargo. Grindley couldn't help but think that if they were unable to make shore, the loss of the *Pollux* could turn out to be a far greater hit to the ranks of the Navy and the families of the crew than to the war effort. Turney decided to try and back off. Her engines squealed. Her propellers flailed in frenzied seas.

After consulting with his executive officer, Lieutenant Commander John Gabrielson, Turney made the decision to hold her aground. "At least the cargo will be salvageable," he said.

Grindley was not so certain. He peered into the murk. The searchlight picked up the grim outline of a sheer wall of rock reaching up behind the protruding ledge, partially concealed under a shifting swath of fog. Making shore would not be easy. A salvage operation could prove even trickier. The *Pollux* was nudged forward, in a fury of heaving and thrashing, to within 20 yards of the ledge.

Grateful wasn't a word Grindley, in the normal course of events, would have associated with their current situation. However, as he noted the unprepared state of the stunned and bedraggled crew congregating on deck (some barefoot, others in shirtsleeves, and practically all without foul weather gear), he was grateful for two things: there had been no loss of life to this point, and the *Pollux* was a supply ship. There would be no shortage of clothing, winter issue in particular.

Gabrielson and the other officers began to initiate abandon-ship procedures. Grindley dispatched his ratings to the crews' quarters with orders to load up on anything deemed useful. In jig time, they were back with supplies needed to survive a few days: food, water, blankets, jackets, boots, even a few bottles of whiskey and the captain's personal supply of smokes. They stashed it all on the port deck. After accounting for the crew and seeing that they were being properly clothed and fed, the officers continued to make their rounds, taking stock of the ship's state.

Waves pounded the *Pollux* and badgered the bulkheads, bleeding into the crews' quarters.

▼▲▼

After a brief pause, Calemmo's brain and body kicked back into gear. They'd need his motor launches.

Sailors swarmed up the ladders, heading for their emergency stations. Calemmo deked a path through to the boats. The diesel in Number One Starboard Launch started on the first try, but the boat see-sawed madly in its cradle. All the boat gripes used to lash the motor launch in place had snapped, the cable ends still attached to their ring bolts on the deck. Not about to be knocked overboard on the next wave, he skedaddled out of there. But before he made it back, a colossal wave walloped the launch, rendering it useless.[72]

Next, Calemmo made his way to Number Two Portside Launch. It was already useless: flooded, his light bulbs pulverized, the diesel

---

72   Brown, *Standing into Danger*, 117.

dead. He swore, but with heavy waves clobbering the foredeck, he didn't dally. Minutes later, the launch was scooped up on a wave and lobbed clear of the ship. He watched it drop into a deep trough. Two boats out of commission.

Calemmo found his lifeboat crew and enlisted their help to chip ice from the canvas covering one of the life rafts. Fighting to stay afoot, they strained to push the heavy balsa wood raft, big enough to hold 15 men, up the icy, slanted deck. They'd get a quarter of the way, sometimes half, and then the *Pollux*'s hull would plunge down on the rocks and knock them off their feet. They'd slide back, to start all over again. It was taking so long that Turney ordered Gabrielson to ready Number Three Motor Launch, hanging in over the deck due to their starboard list, be readied.

Calemmo, struggling with the raft, looked up and saw a boom swinging above his head and sailors using guidelines to control it. He left his crew working on the raft and dodged across the deck to see what was up. A cargo boom was ready to lift the motor launch off its cradle; Chief Machinist Mate Irving Smith was aboard trying, without success, to start the engine.

Calemmo shouted, "I'll take over, Chief."

Smith got out and Calemmo hopped aboard the launch. Under Calemmo's touch, the motor started on the first go. Using the 30-foot cargo boom from number five hold, the crew lifted the boat about 6 feet off the cradle. The boom swung out over the side just as a wave picked up the *Pollux* and plunged her portside on the rocks. The guideline snapped. The boom swayed overhead. The *Pollux* was knocked savagely back on her hull. The crew in the launch executed wild loop-de-loops before swinging back over the deck and crashing into the captain's gig. Somehow, the crew survived, but Number Three Motor Launch and the captain's gig were knocked out of commission.[73]

---

73   Brown, *Standing into Danger*, 132.

Calemmo, recovering his breath, eyeballed the wreckage. "Well, that's two more boats down," he announced to no one in particular.

▼▲▼

"Send a detail forward to assess any damage," Turney ordered Damage Control Officer Stroik.

Shipfitter 1st Class William Stanford, Stroik's assistant, led Califano and another sailor to the storage area of the crew's quarters, two decks below. The racket of the waves hammering the *Pollux*'s iron hull was deafening as was the unmistakable sound of seas surging through Number Three Hold. Stanford shone his emergency light down into the hold. The water was rising fast; in no time, it would flood the crew's quarters.

"Close the watertight doors and dog them down," Stanford ordered.

Califano shut doors on the portside; his mate, the starboard. They passed through the crew's quarters into the mess and shut the watertight doors behind them, dogging them too. Califano knew that the watertight doors would hold only as long as the bulkhead did.

"Phone the information to the bridge," Stanford told Califano. Then, addressing them both, "Stand fast while I go below to the engine room to see how the forward bulkhead plates are holding."[74]

Stanford returned looking grim. The bulkhead plates were starting to bulge at the seams and water had already begun to leak through. Stroik sent a crew to shore them up.

Oddly enough, the galley was open for business. With the ship listing 10 degrees to starboard, and rocking like a cradle in a hurricane, the two cooks, Dusty and Nicosia, served up breakfast as if it were a routine day at sea. Califano did a double take at the incongruous sight, and then, up to his knees in sea water, chowed down on fried eggs and a substantial hunk of ham. Most ate heartily. No one said anything, but

74   Brown, *Standing into Danger*, 121. There is no information available as to which damage-control team Califano was actually on.

all were aware that this meal might be the last bit of grub they would get for a while. Quartermaster Strauss's slice sported an oily fingerprint, but he ate it without saying a word. Califano downed his last bite and headed out on deck.

Word spread fast that the crew's quarters were starting to flood. Some headed below and slogged through oily crud toward their lockers to rescue prized possessions. They grabbed cigarettes, watches, snapshots of family and girlfriends, their precious blues, pints of liquor they'd slipped aboard on a turn down south, and money. Warren Greenfield rescued his beloved guitar that had cost him two months' pay. Califano, with water and oil sloshing at his rear, hesitated. Besides his mother's diamond ring, which he usually wore on a chain around his neck, he had some family snapshots and his tailor-made blues in his locker. He decided to leave everything but the ring.

Back on deck, Califano joined his shipmates who were surveying the shoreline, eyes corroborating what his gut knew. Although they were aground mere yards from shore, the coast stretched out in a flush run of cliffs, except for a huge rock ledge that loomed over the bow, not far shy of spitting distance if a fellow was good.

With the ship disintegrating beneath them, they needed to get to that ledge. Somehow.

▼▲▼

The heavy, grey morning emerged, dragging, revealing the misery borne on a malevolent sea.

Behind the ledge, the cliff stretched straight up for about 75 feet before ending in a rough curve that connected to an overhang at the top. The terrible sounds of the ship clanking on the rocks rumbled off the cliff. Grindley gauged her stern to be about 200 feet offshore. Her starboard side, almost parallel to land and broadside to the raging ocean, bore the brunt of the storm. Portside, the bow practically leaned over the rock ledge. Grindley noted that, while its middle was capped in snow, the sides sloped downward. The ledge's outer edge was laced heavily with layered jags of sea ice and collared by a yellow ring: the high-water mark. At full tide, only the very top would be above water.

The morning light also revealed the compromised situation of the *Wilkes*, aground about a mile west of the *Pollux*. Grindley and Turney kept an eye on the *Wilkes*'s efforts to back off the shelf. Finally, at 0710 hours, she managed to reverse into deeper water. Grindley harrumphed. They should be so lucky.

Turney was relieved—for the war effort. The Navy could not afford the loss of another destroyer. Surveying the extreme devastation pressing in on all sides, he recognized that with the grounding of the *Pollux*, the Navy had lost a supply ship; Turney hoped the *Pollux*'s crew would not be lost too.

The *Pollux* continued with abandon-ship procedures. Grindley supervised Disbursing Officer Ensign Pollack as he stuffed $47,000 into a canvas bag tethered to a float by a coil of rope. Another $38,000 in vouchers were jammed into Pollack's own briefcase.[75] Pollack was ordered to lug the briefcase, bag, and rope everywhere he went. Navy regs. Roughly $1,500 in silver sat in the safe.

"Can I leave the silver, Lieutenant?" Pollack asked.

Grindley's nod was curt. He was sure he heard Pollack grouse. "Let the Navy dive for its nickels and dimes." Grindley was inclined to agree with Pollack.

The officers and their crews shoved navigation records and files into canvas sacks; restricted and secret documents went into heavily weighted bags and then into pillowcases for easier handling. All were piled on deck, along with the main safe, ready to go ashore.

The wind was Force 8; the barometer was still falling, indicating that

---

75   Brown, *Standing into Danger*, 119.

the storm was not over yet. And the tide was rising. Through the early morning hours, the officers continued to check the ship for flooding and damage. For all their best efforts, fuel oil gushed out—turning the channel between ship and shore from dirty yellow to a black scum—and wild water rushed in, flooding Numbers One, Two, and Three Holds (fouling their supply of fresh water), and then reaching up to the deck plates forward.

How long before the ship succumbed to this savagery?

▼▲▼

With four boats already out of commission, Calemmo and his crew returned their attention to the raft they'd abandoned earlier.

The seamen, soaked by freezing spray and badgered by sleet, doubled down on their efforts, working around menacing 100-pound aerial bombs that the seas had broken free.[76] Not fused, they washed back and forth across the deck. Finally, the raft was in position to be lowered. Secured to the ship's railing, it took a beating. Waves falling back from the cliff took it in tow, whipped it at the ship, and sent it crashing against the iron hull. The battering repeated wave after wave after wave.

Bradley, Quartermaster Rex Copeland, and Seaman Bill McGinnis, with the captain's permission, decided to attempt to reach shore. In foul weather gear and tied to lifelines, the three jumped from the cargo net as the raft rose up on a surge of wild water.

Thankfully, all made it aboard. They grabbed the paddles and dug in. However, the strong undertow, combined with rough seas and heavy crude, created a yo-yo effect that sucked the raft back to the ship. The line from the raft to the *Pollux* became tangled in debris and fouled. The men on deck howled when Bradley jumped into the water. They

---

76   Rowsell, *Waves of Courage*, 64.

watched his body twist toward shore, but the strong undertow bore him back to the ship. Calemmo and his mates hauled the three sailors aboard and willed them to life with nips of whiskey and blankets.

All recognized that someone had to make shore before they all floated with the flotsam.

▼▲▼

Califano stamped his feet to keep some life in them.

The crew at the railing were a solemn bunch. Next to Califano, Pollack and Lieutenant James Boundy stood with Dr. Bostic, discussing Bradley, Copeland, and McGinnis's failed attempt to paddle ashore.

"Maybe if they weren't wearing such heavy gear they could move easier and would have had a better chance," Pollack speculated.

Boundy nodded. "Maybe."

Dr. Bostic said nothing.

Out of the blue, Pollack said, "How about we try to swim ashore? It's not far."

Boundy certainly thought so. "I'll do it if you will."

The thought had crossed Califano's mind as well. They knew from training that three or four minutes was the maximum a man could survive in the North Atlantic waters in winter. With adrenaline pumping, and a lucky push from the wind and waves, Pollack and Boundy could make it. Possibly.

Dr. Bostic thought the idea crazy and warned that they would need protection in such frigid waters. Someone offered a can of grease. The two went below, stripped down to swim trunks, greased up, and put on lifejackets. Back topside, Pollack and Boundy paraded to Turney. Their mates, hooting and hollering encouragement, parted on either side to let them through.

"Nice trunks!"

"Perfect day for a swim!"

Pollack and Boundy lapped up the attention. "We'll save you a good spot on the beach," Pollack promised with a wave. He turned to Turney, "Request permission to board the raft and get a line ashore, sir. We'll swim if we have to."

Califano couldn't hear what Turney said to Pollack and Boundy but saw him shake their hands. Beckoning to Califano, Turney said, "Grab that line, the 18-foot one, and secure it to both their lifejackets."

"Jeez, there's no gettin' rid of you now," Boundy joked to Pollack as Califano bound them together on the line.

Both men, known to be strong swimmers, dropped into the raft, ready to launch themselves for the swim of their lives. Immediately, the raft smashed against the ship. Califano cringed. Pollack and Boundy, still aboard, hit water, sank under the surf, and shot back to the surface, sea water streaming off them. Again, the raft was picked up on a wave and smashed against the ship's hull. This time, Pollack and Boundy were thrown overboard.

The crew watched in horror. Bested by the same deadly undertow that had beaten Bradley, Copeland, and McGinnis, Pollack and Boundy too were dragged back to the ship. Califano, along with several other seamen, grabbed a lifeline and began hauling. Together they worked the other line, hoisting the men up the cargo net before the raft could come at them again. Back on board, Dr. Bostic gave them sips of medicinal alcohol. Someone quipped, "You sods will do anything for a drink."

Califano spotted a small band lurching along the deck. Some shouldered two-by-fours; others clutched an assortment of beams. One of them said that Strauss figured they might be able to lay a plank across from the bow to the ledge. Califano was doubtful, but he didn't have a better plan.

Hot behind the sailors trotted Storekeeper Flechsenhaar, responsible for keeping track of that lumber. "Hold up," he squawked, teetering with each roll of the ship, "you can't have that until I write it in the stores' log."

In the end, the planks were a half-baked idea. No one could figure out what to do with them. The boys standing around made jokes about walking the plank. Someone suggested that they construct a see-saw and lob the new recruits across first to test it out. Flechsenhaar was happy; he got his lumber back.

Another bunch tried throwing a grapnel hook to the ledge to establish a line and set up a breeches buoy. The hook was heavy; at best, the boys could lob it only three-quarters of the way before they struck out. The few times it smacked rock, it landed on the sea-buffed outer edge and slid off. After a thousand attempts, the hook caught on a fissure and held. Boatswain's Mate Glen Wiltrout yanked it hard several times. It was solid; the boys were so proud they swaggered. They pulled it taut and Boatswain's Mate Hoot Gibson secured it to the rail.

Strauss volunteered to establish the rope.[77]

Califano thought, and his buddies Machinist's Mate Phillip Jewett and Shipfitter Charles Killelea agreed, that Strauss was the right man for the job. His slight, wiry build wouldn't put too much strain on the rope. And, as Jewett said with a chuckle, "Under that goon jacket he's still greased up and sporting his swim trunks."

Califano laughed. Strauss too had greased up ready to try for shore with Pollack and Boundy but hadn't made it topside in time. He was about to get his chance now.

Reluctantly, Turney, who had been watching, gave permission.

Wiltrout and Gibson attached a line to his lifejacket. "If you can't make the ledge, we'll haul you in," they assured him.

"You'd better!" Strauss replied and grabbed the rope. Hand over hand, he pulled himself across the 60 or 70 yards to the ledge.

---

77   Brown, *Standing into Danger*, 138.

A rapt audience at the railing followed his every move. Califano thought he looked like a daredevil acrobat swinging above those seas.

However, before Strauss could set foot on the ledge, a huge sea wiped his legs from under him and towed him under. They spotted him tumbling in the surf.

On deck, Califano and the boys went into overdrive. Petrified they could lose him, they hauled and hauled but couldn't get a solid grip on the oily cable attached to his lifejacket. Straining. Straining. Getting nowhere. Desperate, Wiltrout tied the tarry rope around his middle and turned in a circle: a human winch. The men spun him, the rope drawing taut as a hawser to a capstan, hoisting the seemingly lifeless Strauss up the ship's side. He opened his eyes as they hauled him over the rail. They lugged him off to sick bay, slipped a few drops of 190 proof down his throat, and gave his limbs a vigorous rubdown. They searched for dry clothing among the supplies being loaded on deck, pawing through piles, throwing curses in all directions. The shot of 190 proof, rubdown, and dry clothing worked like a trick. Strauss trotted back on deck, as if the ordeal had never happened.

"Well, boys, what can we try next?"

Califano figured that if Strauss wasn't giving up, neither was he.

▼▲▼

The *Wilkes* flashed a message at 0803 hours: *Are you getting your crew ashore?*

The *Pollux* flashed back: *We have not been able to get a line ashore yet, but we are endeavouring to.*[78]

Grindley and the team of officers alternated back and forth between assessing the worsening state of the *Pollux* and the men's efforts to make it ashore. With all other attempts having produced no results, a

---

78   Brown, *Standing into Danger*, 132.

few officers on the bridge considered the possibility of using number two cargo boom to reach the ledge.

"It's worth a try," Grindley said. Lightened by the fuel spill, the bow had risen to within 20 feet of the ledge. "The boom is 50 feet long. It should reach shore with no problem."

"There's no power forward," said Bradley, "so the boom will have to be manoeuvred manually."

Grayson added, "That'll work. The men can shinny down a rope ladder to the reef."

The officers nodded their agreement. Close to 0900 hours, with the ship bucking and rolling beneath them, a crew led by Strauss, working under a deluge of waves, began hacking ice off the boom and cradle. Once they could get a grip, they wrestled the 10-ton boom up and out of its cradle. Strauss volunteered to try and reach the ledge. With Turney's permission, Strauss, trailing a lifeline, grabbed the swaying rope ladder attached to the end of the boom and planted his hands and feet on the rungs. Using guidelines, the crew swung the boom out over the sea. Cheered on by the men, he rode the ladder to the ledge, one foot reaching down, ready to drop onto the rock and rig a lifeline. But the officers had miscalculated: the boom fell 3 or 4 yards short. Salty shouts of disbelief and protest studded the air. Strauss and the boom were swung back aboard ship.

The officers put their heads together, desperate to come up with another plan. The forward bulkheads were buckling, further weakening the plates. Water was boarding. Heavier by the minute. Cracks appeared on the forward deck. The stern was taking sledgehammer-like waves. Rocks and waves worked in tandem to tear the ship apart. Before long, their concern would be not how they'd make it ashore.

But *if* they would.

Calemmo, who had not given up on getting a boat across to the cove, turned to another group working a raft up the deck.

Boatswain's Mate Garrett Lloyd hollered to him, "Me, Jack, and Wag are taking Number One Whaleboat ashore. We need you to work the engine."

Calemmo didn't need to be asked twice; he was confident that they could make it ashore in a boat. The three studied the shoreline. They had two options: straight-up cliffs or iced-up slopes. Then Calemmo noticed that, across from the ledge, behind a cradle of rocks, a crooked cut in the cliff carved out a gap. A slight cove. And between the rocks and the cove was a small pool of calmer waters.

Their plan was simple: run her over the rocks, aim for the cove.

▼▲▼

After the attempt with the boom failed, most went in search of dry clothes and shelter. Califano did not.

He was going ashore. One way or another. He looked around, weaved along the listing deck. Starboard, then port. One of the portside whaleboats was still intact under a heavy coat of ice. Califano clambered over the gunwale. He tried the engine. No luck on the first try, or the second. At his third cursed attempt, someone grabbed his shoulder. He looked up to see his pal, Larry Calemmo, standing behind him with several officers.

Calemmo shouted over the gale, "You going somewhere, buddy?"

Delighted to see his pal, Califano said, "Yeah, ashore if I can get her started!"

Calemmo, the engine expert, grinned, "Never mind, we'll take her over," he said, bobbing his head toward the officers.

"Yes, sir!" Califano replied, scrambling out.

Calemmo jumped aboard. Busied himself with the diesel. One

pull. The engine chugged. Purred. He looked up, sporting a silly grin. "We're goin' ashore, boys!"

Califano, for once, couldn't crack a joke.

▼▲▼

Grindley, Gabrielson, and a few other officers were on the bridge with Turney when Lieutenant Jack Garnaus and Lloyd approached Turney and asked for permission to take the whaleboat ashore.

When Captain Turney appeared to be of two minds, Garnaus said, "Sir, it's the only boat left. We have to give it a try."

Grindley nodded in agreement, as did the other officers.

"If you feel you can make it," Turney said reluctantly, and ordered a crew assembled to launch the whaleboat.

Within minutes, the word was out. A growing cluster of seamen gathered portside aft near the whaleboat. The officers kept them back so that the whaleboat crew could prepare. Greenfield had his signals ready. Garnaus and Calemmo huddled by the whaleboat. Calemmo directed Lloyd: "You control the steering. Keep her on course for shore." He grinned. "The throttle and clutch, that's my job."

Garnaus agreed. A sailor handed him a knife. Another tied a light line to his waist so that when they reached shore, they could attach a heavier line to it to haul the crew across. Greenfield, clutching his flags, jumped aboard. Garnaus took the bow, Calemmo the engine, and Lloyd the tiller. It wasn't until they were all in their ready positions when they noticed that Baker William DeRosa had slipped aboard while they were talking. Grindley ordered a crew to ready the whaleboat to launch. Lowering the boat without getting smashed by the massive surges of water free-falling off the cliff was the first challenge.

"Slow and steady," Grindley instructed.

The whaleboat inched down.

"Hold her now," Grindley called. "Wait for the seas to come up."
"Now!"

▼▲▼

The motor fired on the first try, just as Calemmo expected.

Seas swept up the ship's hull, partially flooding the boat. Calemmo revved the engine; if she stalled, they were in trouble. He couldn't engage the clutch until the whaleboat was unhooked from the ship, a chancy job in these ferocious seas. Timing was everything; a man could lose a finger or even a hand. Eyes on each other, Garnaus unhooked the forward hook, Lloyd the aft. On a nod from Lloyd, Calemmo engaged the clutch. They gunned for the cove, with Lloyd fixed on keeping the bow aimed toward shore. Calemmo's prized diesel chugged. Shipping more water, forward and backward they hurtled, garrotted by the insidious undertow. Calemmo felt himself tiring. Greenfield and DeRosa shouted encouragement. Their instinct and training kicked in. Eyes fastened on the little cove, muscles taxed to their limit, the two men fought the suck and pull of the seas, never once considering that they were grossly outmatched.

Then, from behind, a breaker plucked the whaleboat clear out of the water, whipped it past a spray of rocks, and smashed it down on a huge boulder. Before the boat hit rock, Calemmo and Lloyd were tossed over the starboard side into the cove. They surfaced, waist-deep in surf, at the edge of a thick scum that caked their bodies, clogged ears and noses, and caused their eyes to burn and tear. Groping for traction, they grappled with tarry rocks, trying to leverage a hold. Useless Oxfords; no grip in the slime. Lying on their stomachs, they dragged themselves clear of the water. After resting a short spell, they picked themselves up, fully expecting to see their three mates right behind them. But Garnaus, Greenfield, and DeRosa were nowhere in sight.

"I hope they made it," Calemmo said.

Lloyd motioned to the wrecked whaleboat. Beyond the rocks off its portside was a steep upslope. "I wonder if they could have gone up there?" He paused. "They both had knives."

Agreeing to check back, Calemmo and Lloyd, wet to the skin and chilled to the core, went in search of shelter. Both sides of the little cove were lined by huge slabs of rock, layered in ice from base to rim. Above the rim, yet another slab stretched up. Calemmo gestured to a rent in the wall in front of them. Feet like chunks of ice, they shuffled toward it. The cranny was slanted so as to roof a bit of ground, not more than 6 by 10 feet, Calemmo gauged. Though dark and unbearably cold, it did afford some shelter. "I wouldn't exactly call it a cave," he remarked to Lloyd.

Lloyd didn't argue. After a few minutes of rubbing their arms and shaking their legs, he and Calemmo headed off to look outside for their mates.

Calemmo had scraped his hand, enough to bring blood, and his right shoe was gone. Gingerly, he picked his way over the rocks and found it halfway to the shoreline. Still, there was no sign of the other three men. He and Lloyd returned to the water's edge to check for them. They could see the heavily listing *Pollux* and their shipmates at her port railing, looking toward shore. But there was no sign of the three men who had been tossed overboard with them.

What had happened to them?

▼▲▼

Packed tight among the crew on the port railing, Califano held his breath.

Suddenly a colossal wave scooped the whaleboat up, bore it over a scatter of rocks, and flung it down on a massive boulder at the edge of the surf.

Bodies spilled out, crumpling into the spume.

The *Pollux's* hull drummed on the rocks. The wind wailed. The crew buckled, then pulled themselves back up. Eyes swept the surf. Two blackened forms surfaced in the cove. Roars of relief erupted. Then, the other three sailors broke surface on the portside of the whaleboat, under a sloping bluff.

The railing turned into a backslapping party. Their mates were alive. They had made shore.

And Garnaus was carrying a lifeline.

▼▲▼

Most aboard the *Pollux* figured that they had weathered the worst. Help was close at hand. Some of the junior officers even relaxed.

Grindley's seafaring experience had taught him to be more circumspect. After spotting two of the five sailors heading up the rocky shingle, he kept a sharp eye on the other three who had been swept west of the little cove. They too had made it to shore and were beginning to work their way upward. They seemed to be hacking a path. The crew watched their progress. One of the three going up was Garnaus; Grindley could tell by the lifeline trailing down the incline behind him.

Shortly, Lloyd and Calemmo, using hand signals, messaged from the beach. They were okay, but had not seen Garnaus, Greenfield, or DeRosa. From the ship, the signalman flagged that the other three men were making their way up the cliff. Binoculars in hand, the officers scrutinized their ascent. Garnaus, having left his companions trailing, cut his own crude course upward. Halfway up, the rise eased. The grade levelled somewhat and flattened before running up a scarp that slanted at a stiff angle to the clifftop. A good place to warp[79] the line ashore, in Grindley's assessment. Garnaus stopped there; Greenfield and DeRosa caught up with him.

---

79   Warp lines are long lines or ropes that extend from the boat to a fixed object in the distance.

Shipboard, the crew were growing antsy. Grumbling at how long the boys were taking.

"Patience," Grindley cautioned. "Like you, those men are wet, freezing, and fatigued." He paused to let his words sink in. "They may be taking a breather. They may be hurt."

The sailors nodded; Grindley was right. Irritation in check, they settled down to wait. Fifteen minutes went by. Then 15 more before the light line began moving between ship and shore. There were vigorous cheers all around. The mood lifted. Two or three hundred feet of rope snaked up the incline. As the three men on the slope continued to haul on the light line, the crew aboard the ship attached a heavier three-quarter-inch hawser to the other end. Then, the line stopped moving. It lay in the scummy water swelling with crude and goop. Bloated as a dead flounder.

The *Pollux*'s signalman flagged: *Pull in the three-quarter-inch line.*

Greenfield signalled back: *We can't pull. We do not have the strength.*[80]

The *Wilkes*, having seen the three men going up the slope, signalled to ask if the *Pollux* wanted to send a boat across to the flagship. Turney had the signalman flag that the *Pollux* had no boats left. As well, it appeared that the men on shore were not able to help. The lifeline Garnaus had brought ashore had become fouled in wreckage.

Grindley and the other officers tried to come up with a strategy that might take them ashore. Nothing workable emerged. Their plight was fast approaching hopeless.

The crew had become quiet; some drifted back from the railing. Grindley marshalled a group to work on freeing the lifeline, replacing them with a fresh team on the quarter-hour, but with no results. The line was too heavy, too tangled, too cruddy. The cracks on the forward deck continued to widen. The *Wilkes* could offer no assistance.

Turney consulted with his officers. At 0947 hours, the *Pollux* sent a

---

80   Brown, *Standing into Danger*, 146.

message to the *Wilkes: We cannot land men on the beach. Request help be sent from shore. Please transmit.*[81]

There was nothing to do but wait. Patience was not one of Grindley's virtues, particularly when their situation, in his mind, was absolute folly. With a grain of common sense, the whole mess need not have happened.

Shaking it off, he stepped inside to inspect the ship. Again.

▼▲▼

Learning that Garnaus, Greenfield, and DeRosa had gone up the cliff gave Calemmo and Lloyd a lift.

"We should try and follow them," Calemmo urged.

Lloyd agreed. "If we can make it up, we might be able to figure out a way to get help."

They scrutinized the scarp. Calemmo scowled at their chances. Slim to none, he figured. They tried to leverage footholds anyway. Lloyd hoisted Calemmo up. Calemmo slipped and banged his arm in the attempt. Next, they inspected the cave. From one wall, an uneven stretch of jagged rocks extended out to the shoreline of the cove. However, the jut of rock was heavily laced with ice. On a good day, they might be able to make their way around it. But not today. They returned to the raw chill of the cave.

As they lay there, above the din of the *Pollux*'s thuds and rumbles they heard the faint voices of their mates on the *Pollux*. No, impossible that the winds would allow for their voices to carry to land. But Calemmo was sure that he heard them. He stood. The voices were coming from above. They rushed outside and looked up to see Garnaus looking down at them from the top of the cove. The lifeline he had brought ashore trailed down over the cliff and out to the *Pollux*. Calemmo and Lloyd grabbed on and hauled. But the hawser, weighted down by

81   Brown, *Standing into Danger*, 149.

hardened crude and a thick glaze of ice, wouldn't budge. Trying to get a grip, they flung gobs of oil and tangled junk into the surf. Blood ran off the tar, but they could feel nothing. The lifeline, dragged west by the current, was hopelessly tangled. There was no prospect of pulling it ashore.

Unable to communicate with their mates above, and cut off from the *Pollux* with her abundant reserve of food and clothing, Calemmo and Lloyd were stranded in the little cove.

Their rations and emergency supplies were gone—tossed into the surf when they were.

▼▲▼

Califano was part of a crew that Grindley rounded up to work on the hawser that had tangled between ship and shore.

The three-quarter-inch lifeline was more snarled and gummed up than ever. Still, Califano wasn't complaining. At least Grindley was trying. And, in spite of the cutting sleet in his face and vicious gale knifing through him, he felt good doing something while they waited to get off the ship. He finished his stint and stopped to rub some life into his cramped, frozen hands before heading to the railing to check on Calemmo and Lloyd in the cove. He spotted Calemmo standing at the edge of the surf, waving across to sailors hanging on to the port railing. Califano knew that his pal must be near ballistic at the fact that he was ashore and yet not able to get help; Calemmo was no better off than they were on the ship. Califano was thankful that his friend wasn't alone on the shingle. If Garnaus and his mates didn't bring help soon, they'd all be goners.

Clutching his mother's ring, Califano vowed that he wasn't going down without a fight.

▼▲▼

As the tide began to fall, the *Pollux*'s starboard list worsened, though the bulging bulkhead plates were still holding.

All morning long, the cracks on deck had been widening due to the increasingly heavy weight of the flooded forward section. On the bow, Grindley noted a large crack had opened from port clear across to starboard just forward of the bridge. They produced loud, unsettling sounds like offshore ice at breakup—except that it was underfoot.

Generators were shut down. Steam hissed out. The ship was without power. Broken and dead in the water. The *Wilkes* floated life rafts to them. The seas took them.

A Navy plane circled, its trailing line as useless as the tail of a kite. It dipped dangerously low and rose up far too close to the cliffs, in Grindley's mind. A hefty crosswind would slam it into the rock. Better be snappy, he thought. They needed rescue, not reconnaissance.

Turney signalled the *Wilkes*: *Please tell plane to get help from the beach.*[82]

Within minutes, a reply came back. Help would arrive overland in two hours. Two hours! Grindley bristled. The plane flew off, disappearing into the fog. The Navy—too little, too late. He doubted the ship could survive another two hours. Or the men. He cringed at what would happen if the *Pollux* foundered with her crew still aboard. The loss of so many young lives; it was unthinkable, unnecessary. The *Pollux* shifted, shivered, the tremors felt through the deck. Every sailor braced for the worst.

Close to midday, the bow broke off. With a deafening grind, it cleaved away from the destroyer. On a long, drawn-out groan, it skewed to starboard, spewing cargo into the sludge. Its afterpart pounded on the rocks. The hull, leaking badly, would go any time. Grindley knew

---

82   Brown, *Standing into Danger*, 166.

that all that remained was for her to slide under. Officers rushed about, bellowing orders. Seas mounted the ladders, rung by rung, at an alarming speed. The stern swung onto the portside rocks. Then another grinding list to starboard. Then another.

From the starboard side, seas surged aboard, and the starboard plates buckled. Turney, after hastily consulting his officers, passed the word that anyone willing to swim had permission to do so. He stood by, eyes watery. His lips moved in prayer.

Grindley decided to wait it out. He wasn't ready to abandon ship yet.

He'd see what happened in the next little while. He watched the men slide down the ropes or drop from the cargo nets. There must have been 100 or more. His heart, his gut, went with them.

The starboard searchlight went under, making up the minds of wavering sailors. The sights Grindley witnessed from the railing of the *Pollux* that February morning would remain with him always. Boys, many as young as 18, jumped into the morass of congealed oil. Some tried to crawl back up the cargo net after thinking twice about their decision, but they were pulled under. The shrieking wind keened with the calls of drowning men crying for help.

Grindley passed a shaky hand over his eyes.

▼▲▼

Calemmo roved the shoreline for anything useful washing ashore.

Lloyd was the first to see them. "Larry, they're going over the side!"

"Holy mackerel! Here they come, Lloyd!"

The *Pollux*'s broken bow hung heavy to starboard. Practically under water. Men streamed over her side in a concentrated wave of orangey black torsos.[83]

Spilling down the cargo nets.

---

83   Brown, *Standing into Danger*, 169.

Slipping down lifelines.

Jumping from the railing.

Dropping into the dreck.

Calemmo and Lloyd witnessed their shipmates die before their eyes. The raft the crew had attempted to take ashore, still secured to the ship, twisted maniacally in the gale. A half-dozen sailors jumped to it from the cargo net. A few managed to drop into the raft on their own; others were pulled in by mates. The raft rode up a vertical wall of water before dropping into a deep trough, dispatching the sailors in a freefall.

Calemmo and Lloyd swore ripe oaths when life jackets, hauled on in a hurry, flew off and skittered across the surface of the water like grimy orange seagulls. Other sailors had not properly secured the chin straps. The force of the water on impact pushed the life jackets upward, jamming their arms straight up over their heads. They were pulled under, trapped by gear meant to save their lives.

Sailors at the railing chucked overboard anything the men could grab: crates, paddles, buoys. All added to the wreckage swirling about— and to the likelihood of sailors being hit in the head by rescue devices weaponized by gale-force winds and heavy seas. Calemmo doubled over in alarm when he saw a paravane hit the water. A paravane! Incredulous, he watched as the torpedo-shaped device with serrated teeth at its front end to sever mine moorings zipped about on the waves, orbiting in and out among men already battling for their lives. He stared, unable to drag his eyes away. The paravane zipped about in a psychotic frenzy until the slick clamped on to it.

"I'd like to have 30 seconds with the numbskull who thought it was a good idea to chuck that overboard," Calemmo shouted over the racket to Lloyd.

Some sailors being swept toward them in the cove grabbed the gummed-up lifeline Garnaus had left dangling down the cliff and across the water and pulled themselves hand over hand toward shore. Heavy seas sluicing between the rock and the ledge prevented Calemmo and Lloyd from wading out to reach their mates, so the two men edged forward on their stomachs, linking arms with any who still had breath and the will to live and dragged them ashore. One sailor latched on to Calemmo, his vicelike grip digging into Calemmo's arm. As Calemmo began to pull him toward shore, he felt the sailor's clutch loosen as his last ounce of energy drained away. Calemmo shouted at him but the sailor had no fight left. Unable to goad the guy into helping himself, Calemmo had to let go and move on to the next fellow.

His swearing and shouting worked on McCarron though. Calemmo called the Irishman every name he had in his robust, sailor vocabulary. Finally, he got a rise. McCarron lunged at him and landed out of the surf. Calemmo would have grinned, except he was bereft of the energy to do so. The sailor owed him a drink—if they ever saw a pub again. Right now, they needed to get these fellows to the shelter. He and Lloyd badgered their sorry carcasses, herding them as they crawled on all fours, up over the rocks, hauling, shoving, swearing until 18 sailors huddled inside the ice-cold cranny.

Looking at his shipmates, shivering, shaking, Calemmo figured that all together they weren't able to generate as much heat as one of the light bulbs he'd installed aboard his motor launches. There were still lots more of their shipmates out there past the rocks. Calemmo could only hope they'd make it to shore. He wondered about Califano. He was a Brooklyn brat. Tough. Scrappy.

Calemmo decided that his pal would make it.

When the starboard searchlight went under, Califano knew that his ship was going down. And he was going over the side.

He decided against the see-sawing cargo net. He didn't want to get hung up behind a logy fellow or get a foot tangled and bash himself to death against the *Pollux*'s iron hull. Instead, he decided to take the lifeline. It'd be faster, and he'd have a better chance of clearing the ship before she rolled under—provided there was a shred of luck floating around. The officers were attaching more lifelines to the railing. Califano found himself caught up in the rush—a sailor practically had to take a number to go over the side. Good thing there were a bunch of lines. And a good thing those going over didn't drag their feet about it. Adrenaline ran as high and fast as the seas.

Pete Manger waved a hand and slid down the rope. Bob Collins did the same before he disappeared. Califano, right behind him, saluted the *Pollux* one last time. The boys ahead of him let go of the line about halfway and sank into deep troughs. Not Califano. He intended to delay the shock as long as he could. He grabbed hold and trapped the lifeline between his legs, cautiously easing his way down until the waves lashed at his knees. Eyes riveted shoreward, he let go, muscles fired, arms stretched out ready to swim. Before he could kick off, a breaker bowled him over and somersaulted him deep into the undertow. The frigid waters seeped underneath his foul weather gear, sending ice water through his veins and drilling directly into every nerve ending in his body. Shocked, he corkscrewed around and bobbed to the surface, grateful for his life jacket.

He faced the *Pollux*'s hull. Some of the men tried to swim back through the sludge to the cargo net. Within minutes, they succumbed. Others crawled up a few rungs of the ladder only to be knocked backward by a wave into the spume. Still others, thrown against the ship, fell lifeless into the flotsam. Califano looked away, but there was no escaping the dead and dying mates tossing about in the thundering surf, their pitiful wails for mothers, for God, for help, rising on the wind. Help that would not be coming, he knew. An acrid fear gripped him. He couldn't think, couldn't breathe, couldn't move his limbs.

"Breathe. Calm," he repeated aloud to himself, when calm was the last thing he felt and his breath was being pounded out of him. "Breathe. Calm." The words penetrated his brain and lessened the fear, tamping it down a notch. If he were going to make shore, it would be by his own doing. That certainty cleared his mind, sharpened his focus. He filled his lungs, retched on the stench and the vile taste of crude, and fought to roll over. Arms flogging the surf, face and eyelashes caked in crud, he turned toward shore.

Struggling against the strong westerly current proved useless; his efforts got him nowhere. And he was tiring fast. A voice in his head said, *Go with it. Not against it.* He stopped his attempts to swim and instead let the scummy flow take him diagonally toward the rocks. In his peripheral vision, he was vaguely aware of a few others doing the same. He worked his way around debris bunged up at the edge of the slick where the tarry oil had collected, forming a layer of thick gel that slightly tamped down the wave action. Heavy surf hammered the rock ledge sticking out from shore, burying the sides in dirty yellow spume; he knew he'd never be able to crawl up there.

He grabbed a crate: eyes burning, gooped-up eyelids drooping. A rest was what he needed. Just a few minutes. Suddenly, the crate slipped out from under him and knuckled the side of his head. Hard enough to stir his senses. *Hypothermia*—the word as bold in his mind as it had been on the page in his textbook. His training kicked in: Get as much of the body above water as possible. Stay awake.

Hyper alert now, he dredged up his last ounce of energy. Eyeballing the ledge, he let the heavy seas take him, gambling that the rolling waves would carry him toward the rock ledge—in one piece, he prayed. Mad seas hefted him high, drove him with the calculated viciousness of a schoolyard bully onto a rock at the base of the cliff.

He was half-dead—but half-alive.

Garnaus, Greenfield, and DeRosa, after making their way up the bluff, secured the lifeline and then took shelter in a clump of trees.

While scouting the headland for a way to ferry the *Pollux*'s men to shore, Garnaus encountered Seaman 1st Class William Heldt and Seaman 1st Class Hubert Greene, who had swum ashore and come up the slope the same way Garnaus, Greenfield, and DeRosa had. Garnaus took them to the clump of trees before leaving again to scout the area. On the way, he met local miner Lionel Saint, who had hiked from Chambers Cove to the site to investigate the origin of an oil slick drifting toward the cove. Lionel informed Garnaus that the *Truxtun* too was aground, and veered off to look at the *Pollux* while Garnaus collected the other four men. They forced DeRosa—lying in the snow and close to unresponsive—to his feet and helped him along. With Lionel in the lead, the five men started the three-hour hike to Iron Springs.

The wreckage of the *Pollux* off Lawn Head.

Before long, with DeRosa barely able to walk, Garnaus decided to go ahead with Lionel and bring help. Heldt and Greene, fearing that they too would succumb to the cold, followed, leaving Greenfield with DeRosa. Greenfield helped DeRosa through the drifts until he fell, unable to be revived. Fearing for his own life, Greenfield walked on alone. He arrived at Chambers Cove and told a Navy corpsman that he had left a buddy behind in the bush. The corpsman injected him with morphine and put him on a sleigh. Along the way, Heldt and Greene climbed on the sleigh as well and arrived at Iron Springs not long after Lionel and Garnaus. At the mine house, the men were cleaned up; Heldt was also given a morphine shot.

Later that afternoon, both Heldt and Greenfield were taken to the home of Howard and Isabel Farrell.

CHAPTER 6
ST. LAWRENCE

The girls delivered their last load of supplies to a mine truck and headed home.

Ena had barely closed the porch door behind her when her brothers Aubrey and Cecil pushed it open again.

She gaped at the four sailors with them. They looked about her age, eyes mere slits, with gobs of oil sticking to their lashes and more plastering their hair. Through chattering teeth, the sailors introduced themselves: John Brollini, Arthur Perrault, Stanislaus Kendzierski, who quickly added, "Everyone calls me Ski." The last in, shaky and nervous, leaned against the doorway and stammered his name: John Shields. To Ena, he looked to be in shock.

Aubrey put an arm around him. "Let's get you fellows cleaned up," he said, linking with the sailor through the kitchen and upstairs to the bathroom. Cecil steered a second sailor to a chair in the hallway and sponged him while waiting for the tub to free. Ena ran for towels and blankets. Her mother filled a washbasin and set it on a kitchen chair. The remaining two sailors sat and scrubbed at the crude on their hands and faces while waiting their turn in the tub. They weren't helpless, Ena noted. Cleaned up a bit, she could see that their faces, hands, and ears were blotched white with frostbite. After a good scrub and mugs of hot sugary tea and toast smeared with bakeapple jam, all four were put to bed.

Aubrey and Cecil, having been at Chambers Cove all morning, changed into dry clothes and lay down for a nap; one stretched out on the daybed in the kitchen, the other on the front room couch. While they slept, Ena helped clean up the reeking mess left behind by the sailors before preparing lunch, moving quietly, though she was sure that even the blaring foghorn wouldn't wake them. She boiled a dozen eggs for egg salad sandwiches. Her mother sliced a whole loaf of homemade bread, freshly baked that morning, while Ena buttered it and spread it with spoonfuls of egg salad. "Run to the pantry," she told Ena, "and bring the tin of date squares, and I think there's still some molasses buns too, in the red tin below the pickle jars."

Three hours later, Aubrey was sent to wake the sailors. Howard had phoned to say that the Navy was picking up able-bodied survivors and taking them to the USS *Brant*, and Ena's mother wanted them to have something in their stomachs before they left.

The four sailors trod tentatively down the stairs, brightening at the sight of food. When there wasn't a crumb left on any plate, Cecil herded them into the front room. "Pull your chairs up to the fire," he instructed.

The American sailors, warm, dry, with full stomachs, had mostly recovered. Glad to be alive, they settled back and told their tragic story.

The Farrells listened, hearts breaking for these youngsters. And the unfortunate ones still in the cove.

▼▲▼

Most of the rescuers had come ashore. However, a few miners stayed out in the breakers.

If the handful of sailors clinging to the ship's rail decided to make the leap—before the ship did it for them—the miners would be there to guide them to shore. Amid the commotion caused by pounding surf and men crying for help, the miners on the shingle heard cries coming from a sailor stranded offshore on a sunker. The tide was falling, widening the stretch of beach, but heavy seas persisted. Between onslaughts, the sailor shouted for help, legs flailing every time the sea tried to take him. Gus winced.

Miner Henry Lambert, who for hours had been part of the rescue efforts from the water, scravelled ashore. Gus watched as he tugged on the line trailing down the cliff, signalling that he wanted to be hauled to the top. Gus wondered what Henry was up to. Minutes later Henry, with a coil of rope hooked over his shoulder, was lowered back down. He clambered over the rocks and jumped down into the breakers. After hitching the rope around his middle, he wound up and threw the other end to the marooned sailor. Gus held his breath. The sailor caught it, and Henry hauled him ashore. He hefted the sailor onto his back, plodded through the muck[84] and tied himself and the seaman to the rope hanging down the cliff. The two were hauled up together.

Soon after, Henry was lowered to the shingle again. "Adam Mullins is at the top with a dory," he told Pop.

"A dory?" Pop repeated, looking doubtful. "How's he going to launch a dory in those seas?"

Henry shrugged. "He says he can do it. They're waiting up top for the seas to calm enough to lower it."

Pop and Gus both looked up, scanning the rim of the cove.

Finally, low tide widened the shingle. Around 2 p.m., a dozen men on the rim eased the dory down the scarp. Gus watched, nerves twitching with every dip and cant. His breath seized in his chest when the gale gusted up and threatened to slam it broadside to the cliff. With a few feet left to go, Adam and his crew[85] grabbed the gunwales and guided the dory to the beach. Feeling Pop's eagle eye on him, Gus stayed out of the way, but hovered nearby in case the men needed something. The four men pushed the dory across the shingle. Howard

---

84   Gus Etchegary, telephone conversation with author, August 2018.
85   Adam Mullins, Dave Edwards, Charlie Pike, and Howard Kelly.

Kelly gripped the stern rope and dug in the heels of his rubber boots. Adam and the others boarded. Charlie Pike and Dave Edwards rowed.

The final three men aboard the *Truxtun* clung to the railing.

The dory lurched alongside. Adam threw a line. A sailor caught it and secured it to the ship's rail just as a huge comber broke over the hull and crashed down onto the dory, setting it on end. The dory sank and righted itself—swamped. The oars gone. Adam and Dave were still aboard. Charlie had pitched out and was clinging to the side. One sailor had washed into the dory.[86] Another slumped against the ship's rail.[87] The third man was gone.

Near up to the gunwales in sea water, without an oar, and Charlie barely hanging on, Adam signalled to Howard to haul them back. He said later that the hardest decision of his life was to leave that sailor stranded on his sinking ship. Alone. Surrounded by a sea of dead mates.

However, that last sailor aboard was not about to go down with the ship. Grabbing the light rope tied to the rail, hand over hand he trailed the dory to shore as Adam payed out the line.[88] He made it, but then the surf hurled him up the beach and flung him senseless on the rocky shingle. Face down in noxious crude.

▼▲▼

Clara, Pauline, and Mary followed a trail of oil to the cove.

They strode past the brook, looking like it would burst its banks any minute, and past the blackened hay shed off to the right, eyes peeled for the last survivor. The one Father Thorne said had come ashore on the dory line. Clara crested the gully, Pauline and Mary in tow. "That must be him," she said, pointing to the figure floundering across the

---

86   Edward McInerney, Fireman 2nd Class.
87   Later identified as Donald Fitzgerald.
88   Farrell, *St. Lawrence and Me*, 50, has a reprint of Dr. Warren S. Smith's unpublished account of the February 1942 rescue effort, entitled "The Truxtun & Pollux Disaster."

barrens, propped up by a man on either side. As the women neared, the sailor's head lolled sideways, his legs buckled, and his body sagged to the ground.

From some deep place within, Clara let out a feral mother cry. Something between a sob and sharp pain. She ran to him, fell to her knees, and cradled his head in her arms. The men could not bring him to. Pauline and Mary screeched across the gully to Jack Lundrigan on the other side with his horse and sleigh. Under Clara's watchful eyes, they loaded him on the sleigh. The men told Jack that a search party from a Navy ship docked in the harbour had stopped at Chambers Cove on their way to Lawn Point. Another ship had gone aground.

"Dear God," Mary croaked. "That can't be possible."

Clara shut it out, her attention on the young seaman before her. The women followed close behind the sleigh as it made its way to the mine house. Clara was terrified that they would think that the unconscious man was already dead and wouldn't try to revive him before she got there. She hurried down the path and arrived at the mine house to see him laid out on a table, with Theo and Nurse Ash ministering to him.[89] Clara flew across the room, coat flapping, stuffing her scarf in a pocket.

Theo had just arrived at Iron Springs from the cove. "When I applied pressure to his back," he said, "I felt him spasm. So he's alive."

Nurse Ash added, "At first we thought he was dead. But I was able to get a slight heartbeat. Very faint though."

Theo tried to prise open the sailor's jaws to release his protruding swollen and bleeding tongue. Pauline and Mary tucked hot bricks close to him and rubbed his limbs, but with no success. Clara added another blanket and kept up a constant gentle chatter, assuring him he was going to be okay. She stroked his forehead and cradled his cold hands in hers. This young man was going to make it.

Dusk darkened the windows; the filthy, stinking room resembled

---

89   Turpin, telephone conversation with author, October 8, 2020.

a war zone. All but a few semi-conscious survivors had been taken to town. Howard asked if anyone could take the last survivors home for the night.

Clara swaddled her inert, young man in blankets and climbed into the back of a company truck with the stretcher.

▼▲▼

At the Farrell home that afternoon, the survivors, warm and fed, quickly recovered. Ena went to the piano, Cecil picked up the violin.

Soon other survivors, able to get out around the neighbourhood, stopped in until about 20 were sitting on the floor around the fireplace, singing.[90] A fellow from Texas played the guitar. After flexing his cramped fingers and making fists—to loosen them up he said—he strummed "Deep in the Heart of Texas." Between songs, the room quieted and their spirits sagged. Ena and Cecil did their best to keep the atmosphere upbeat. She tried a few bars of popular American songs until she hit on one that most of them knew and could join in. In the corner, one young sailor, still in shock, cried softly.

Howard Farrell and his wife, Isabel, arrived with two more survivors.[91] Howard, acting mine manager while Donald Poynter was in New York, was headed to the pier for a meeting aboard the *Brant* to put together a rescue plan for the *Pollux*. The *Brant,* a minesweeper, and the tug USS *George E. Badger* had left Argentia as soon as they'd gotten the *Wilkes*'s message in the early morning hours. They docked in St. Lawrence harbour after the eight-hour trip across Placentia Bay. Their crews, guided by St. Lawrence men, were already on the way overland to the wreck sites to offer assistance, Howard told them.

Twitching in frustration, Ena eyed her Brownie camera on the

---

90   Brown, *Standing into Danger*, 247
91   Warren Greenfield and William Heldt from the *Pollux*, who had walked from Lawn Point to Iron Springs with Lionel Saint.

sideboard. "I should have been out there with my camera," she blurted. "That's history in the making."

Howard looked at her. "Why weren't you?"

It was too late to go to Chambers Cove today, but Ena wanted to be ready for the morning. She grabbed her camera and extra roll of film and put it in her knapsack.

▼▲▼

The last of the survivors had gone up the cliff, as had most of the rescuers.

The half-dozen or so men remaining on the shingle trawled through the knee-high crude, checking and rechecking every bulge in case a body had been missed on the first round. Gus gathered up boots, lifejackets, caps, coats, several sets of keys. The saddest were wallets that had been in the water all day. They spilled sodden, grainy snapshots of mothers and wives and girls. He laid them on a Navy blanket up the beach below the overhang.

Mick Turpin was rubbing his back. Pop looked done in. As did every man there.

Gus grabbed the line behind Pop and worked his way back up the cliff, straddling the rope. Halfway up, he spotted Theo's tarry jacket on the ground. Too tired to pick it up, they left it. Along the fence, the bodies were laid out. Some young fellows were covering them with whatever was at hand: pieces of canvas, grubby blankets, and grubbier scraps of clothing.

Gus made the sign of the cross before dragging himself to the rim for one last look below. Chambers Cove would never be the same. Not to him—not to anyone here today.

▼▲▼

Truxtun lies on her side.

The truck jounced over humps and dips in the dirt road.

Kneeling on an old tarp, Clara braced herself and the stretcher. She was petrified that the poor boy wouldn't survive the drive. Ella and Carmel were at the window waiting when Clara pulled up. Ella opened the door wide for the stretcher. On their mother's orders, they pushed the kitchen daybed close to the wood stove. The driver and his helper eased the unconscious sailor onto it. Clara opened the oven door. A robust blast of heat funnelled into the room, and the young man began to shake. The girls and their four younger siblings, Patrick, Fluorina, Madeleine, and Margaret Rose, stood by, uncommonly quiet and solemn in the face of the spectacle in their kitchen.

"Put the children to bed, and then pray the Rosary for him," Clara said to Ella and Carmel.

When their task was completed, the girls knelt by the kitchen table. It was Lent, and Ella began the first Sorrowful Mystery. Besides, this was a sorrowful thing that had happened. Throughout the evening, Clara and her girls tended to their patient. Clara cut up an old blanket. Carmel and Ella dabbed the rags in camphorated oil heated in bowls and plates on the back of the stove and wiped at the crude slathering the unconscious sailor's hands and arms. Clara wrapped her one hot water bottle, even the pans used to warm the oil, in towels and tucked them around him. She scalded her darning needle in the bubbling kettle and lanced blisters the size of beach rocks on his shins. Then she gently patted Mecca Ointment on the open wounds and bandaged them. The older boys, Alex and Gus, arrived home from the Cove, subdued. For once, they had little to say. They too kept vigil with her into the wee hours.

Around 4 a.m., Clara sent the girls to bed. She stayed by her patient's side and comforted his ravings. From time to time, he thrashed about, struggling to speak. During one of his bouts of rambling, he called for his mother and repeatedly uttered the name Jessie May Fitzgerald. Clara understood that he wanted her to let his mother know he was alive. She assured him that she would. That seemed to soothe him. He slept in fits and starts, waking from time to time and sipping a hot tea. In a lucid moment, she learned his name: Donald, he had rasped. Donald Fitzgerald. She was pleased with how he was coming along and told him so.

It wasn't until 9:30 a.m. that Patrick came home from Lawn Head and fell into bed. Then Mrs. Slaney arrived to help. She roused Alex and Gus. They got Fitzgerald on his feet and between them, linked arms with him and walked him around the room to restore his circulation.

Fitzgerald was so grateful. He wanted to give them something and would not rest until he did. He insisted on gifting Carmel with the signet ring from his finger. To mollify him, Clara let her take it, but she would not budge when he wanted to give the boys the $19 in pay he had in his pocket.[92]

Close to 11 a.m., Theo and Alan showed up at the door asking if she would take in another survivor, this time from the *Pollux*.

---

92   Turpin, telephone conversation with author, October 8, 2020.

She would.

Harold Brooks, in one shoe and stone blind from the smoky fire, hobbled into the kitchen. Clara and Mrs. Slaney filled the galvanized tub and scrubbed him until they removed the worst of the oil. The poor boy still couldn't see. Clara pulled the couch from the front room into the kitchen next to Fitzgerald and led the new arrival to it. Clara, drawing on her experience as a midwife, put drops in Brooks's eyes: silver nitrate, like she used on babies to prevent conjunctivitis.

Brooks slept for four hours, and when he woke, his eyes had begun to clear. "I can see you," he cried, "you look just like I thought you would."

Clara chuckled and administered more drops.

In the afternoon, the Navy came to collect Fitzgerald and Brooks and take them aboard the *Brant*. Brooks had recovered, his sight intact, but Fitzgerald still needed nursing.

Clara refused to let him go.

"He's not well enough," she said. "Come back tomorrow."

▼▲▼

It was almost noon the next day—Thursday—before Ena managed to get away. She, Julia, and Ethel would go to Chambers Cove today, and Lawn Head tomorrow.

On her way out the door, she recalled Howard saying that the Navy was picking up able-bodied sailors. She tripped back to the front room and asked the four sailors if they would pose for a snapshot. It was her first time using her camera, and she couldn't have asked for a better reason.

The weather was much improved. Sunny. Clear. Cold. Though skiing conditions weren't great, like a skating rink in places from the sleet yesterday. Ena was a good skier, thanks to having had to keep up with her brothers when she was growing up. They'd skied on worse days. While she waited for the girls to catch up with her, she veered left away from the cove path and pointed her skis toward the mine. There wasn't a soul in the yard. No trucks either.

A few minutes later, Julia and Ethel caught up. "Look at the streels of oil on the snow," she said, trying to catch her breath.

Ena laid her mitts and poles on a hummock. "From the sailors," she said. "The ones at our house were covered in it." She shrugged off her knapsack and pulled out her camera.

"Why are you taking snaps of the mine house?" Ethel asked.

"Because this is where the shipwrecked sailors were brought—like a first aid station." Ena replied. "I want to document the whole thing."

The narrow path was glare ice in spots, in other places blown in so completely they had to skirt around and pick it up again farther on. They took their skis off before they reached the brook, stashed them in a clump of prickly juniper, and slogged uphill, trying to steer clear of the gobs of oil pocking the incline. But with slips and falls, in no time all three had gunky smudges on their clothing. Efforts to wipe the oil off with handfuls of snow only smeared it around.

Ena, slightly ahead, looked down at the old tilt at the bottom of the gully. A mangled, grotty, black trail snaked down the far side of the gully to the tilt.

"They didn't take the path," Ethel said.

"They didn't know where in the world they were, never mind finding a path in the storm," Ena replied. "It's a miracle they didn't walk right off the cliff." She shuddered at the thought. It boggled her mind how the American sailors had managed to make it through those waves while it was blowing a blizzard and then climb an icy cliff to go for help.

Ena slid down the incline, heels ruddering her descent, knapsack cradled in front to protect her camera. She took no pictures. It wouldn't be right. Not until they knew what was inside. The girls followed, picking their way down, grabbing a scattered rock for leverage.

Near the tilt, the trodden-down snow was a stinking yellowy brown mash. Closer in, a sticky mat of black tar overlaid it, the smell so putrid that the girls gagged. Even the boards around the gaping door frame wore thick tar, having collected crude sheared off the sailors like sheep's wool on a wire fence. The girls listened. There wasn't a stir. The only sound was the wind hammering the tilt with the muster of a battering ram, moaning through the spaces between the rough palings. Keening around the corners, as if wise to what had happened here.

Ena, peeking inside, felt the deadly cold of the tilt. Disgusting crude from the door frame graze her cheek. The foul smell in the confined space seared her nostrils and left her slightly woozy. She blinked until she could make out walls, a filthy floor, and pooks of blackened hay. A pall of oil overlaid everything. A bloated lump of crude concealed a life jacket, another buried an arctic boot. She stepped back. Into breath. Into life. Neither girl spoke. A heaviness engulfed them. Like the shifting gale, the afternoon had veered from adventure to tragedy.

Truxtun pieces on the beach.

Ena walked back clear of the sludge. She fiddled with her camera, focused, and clicked. She snapped a few more from a different angle, before tackling the gully.

At the top, the girls looked down on the broken destroyer, all but buried under a welter of waves. Only its forward section, keeled over on its side and jammed up against a huge black rock, remained above water. Ena snapped a few more pictures in the dull evening light, the backdrop a dismal swirl of ashen sky and sea, the foreground cliffs and cove cloaked in a shroud of crude. As doleful a sight as anyone could imagine.

Rescuers in Chambers Cove hauling the decoder up from the wreckage of the *Truxtun*.

Along a stretch of leaning wire fence, bodies were laid out in sombre rows on funereal black snow. In the summertime, she'd barely noticed that fence—the remains of an old sheep farm. From that point on, the image of it would live in her.

A burial ground for young men, many of them about her age, and a far-off war that had become very real.

Father Thorne prays over sailors.

Bodies delivered by boat.

Pulling a casket from Chambers Cove.

Ena Farrell.

CHAPTER 7

USS POLLUX, LAWN HEAD

Ash Wednesday Mass had just finished. Joe Manning headed down the harbour to the slipway to check on his skiff.

He was anxious to see how she had weathered the storm. He was in the habit of leaving her out all winter, and most likely she'd need some cleaning up. Along the road, he met two young fellows from Webbers, Ken Roul and Dolph Jarvis, driving an ox and sleigh. They reined in, and Ken told him, "There's a ship ashore on Lawn Point."

"The biggest kind of steamer! We could see the sea between her and the land," Dolph chimed in.[93]

Manning didn't believe them. How could they have seen a ship 2 miles off when the weather was so thick? He could hardly see across the harbour. But they insisted. Ken said that while he was out getting firewood, something caught his eye on the other side of the harbour; the snow had slackened, and he could see that it was a ship. Dolph was waiting for the weather to clear to go gunning when he spotted what looked to him like flares—all colours of flares—on the horizon. When the squall eased up, he too could make out a ship on Lawn Head.[94]

Shortly after, the telephone switchboard in Lawn lit up with the news from St. Lawrence: An American destroyer aground. In Chambers Cove. Then, around noon, the village buzzed with another report: A second ship ashore. This one on Lawn Point.

Manning reasoned that the ship the boys saw from Webbers, on the

---

93   Joseph Manning to Gerald Ryan, letter, March 31, 1942, MG956.187, The Rooms Provincial Archives of Newfoundland and Labrador.
94   Rowsell, *Waves of Courage*, 74.

west side of Lawn Harbour, must be standing by the one on the rocks. And with Chambers Cove not even 2 miles by sea from Lawn Head, it would swing up around the Point every now and then.

It was the only thing that made sense to him.

▼▲▼

Over 100 men had gone over the *Pollux*'s side. Upward of 80 had died within minutes.[95]

Their helpless bodies, bashed about in the surf, were either taken out to sea or smashed against the rocks. Or against the *Pollux*'s hull. On deck, Turney, his officers, and his crew stood by, mesmerized by the brutality of the fight; their eyes pinned on the few sailors attempting to make shore. Grindley trained his binoculars on the ledge, running a rough tally of the men he saw there. Passing the binoculars to Turney, he said, "I can see close to a dozen on the rock at the far end of the ledge." Then he pointed to the left of the ledge. "The current has taken another 20 or so into the cove."

Turney scanned the coastline on the slim chance that there were still more survivors. Then the winds veered around. The seas shifted, setting her back up on a more even keel—the stability offering the small reprieve of more time. Tears mingled with the sea water on Turney's face. He passed the order to his officers: "Have the men cease attempts to swim."

What now? Grindley wondered. Though rescue was as near as the stark cliffs looming over them, their chances of making shore were bleak. No help from the Navy. Flying recon—not rescue. Nor from the crippled *Wilkes*, not in these seas. Calemmo and Lloyd were trapped at the base of the cliff. The lifeline Garnaus had brought ashore remained useless.

---

95   Brown, *Standing into Danger*, 176.

However, Garnaus, Greenfield, and DeRosa, having successfully scaled the bluff, were alive and scouting the area, as far as he knew. Grindley's concern, and that of the officers, was whether they could survive in their severely compromised state—wet, frozen, with no supplies and marginal shelter—long enough to find help. And even if they did, how long would it take to mount a rescue overland?

He and the officers rallied the crew. For hours, they had tried to get a line to the men who had swum ashore and were stranded on the ledge. Luck was against them there too. Each rope they tried was either too short, too heavy, or snatched by the gale. In a flash of insight, Grindley remembered that he'd bought a fishing line on one of the islands during a turn down south. He ducked inside, retrieved it, and looking around for something weighty, he spotted the TBS receiver. He yanked it from the cable and attached it to the fishing line for heft.

"Let this work," he said, swinging it over his head like a lasso.

▼▲▼

In the cove, Calemmo and Lloyd kept their 18 mates mobile.

"No one, *no one* is gonna fall asleep on my watch," Calemmo drilled into their dulled brains. For added emphasis, he singled out the boys he knew. "Ya hear that, Mongeau?" He waited for Mongeau's reply.

"Got it," Storekeeper Phillip Mongeau mumbled.

"Hanson? You understand what I'm sayin'?"

Storekeeper Hanson bobbed his head, his whole frame shuddering with the cold.

Satisfied, Calemmo nodded to Lloyd, who ordered the men to pair up and try to find a way up the cliff. Lloyd too was blunt. "If your mate goes down, you're to summon help."

Having already tried, Calemmo knew that finding a way up was highly unlikely, but hell, these guys didn't know that. The exercise kept them moving, kept a sliver of hope alive. The whole lot were in rough shape. Most had lost caps and gloves to the seas they'd come through, not that they'd be any use soaked through and turning to ice. Standing in front of him in various pathetic states of dress, in soggy shoes or shoeless altogether, the boys shook as if possessed. Calemmo would give his last smoke to be near the stash of winter issue weather gear that he knew was piled on the *Pollux*'s deck. His eyes lit on a fellow crippling across the rocks in one shoe. Behind him slogged another sailor—a purple swollen foot slipping in and out of the other shoe.

Blasted by wind and sleet, Calemmo and Lloyd had the men test every gap, every crack, clump, and fissure for finger holds, toeholds— for anything that might give them a leg up. Their efforts produced nothing but skinned knees, shins, and scraped hands and feet. The boys had already suffered enough; not wanting to inflict more pain on them, Calemmo had them shout up the cliff instead. Only the echoes of their own voices came back.

Hoarse and disheartened, they limped and crawled back to the coldness of the cave.

▼▲▼

Califano had lost one of his shoes. It wasn't until he tried to lever himself up higher on the rock that he'd realized it.

Several on the rock with him had lost both. He felt numbness, but no pain, and was grateful for that small mercy. For the past two hours, he and a few semi-alert survivors had been trying to catch the line from the *Pollux*. When the gale didn't take it, the surf did. Melvin Bettis crept forward as far as the slick rime edging the rock. He reached for the rope, slipped, and saved himself only by grabbing a chunk of ice as he began to slide. After that, the men had no heart for it.

They slumped back down on the rock and curled up to conserve energy. Califano thought he heard something above the racket manufactured by the rough weather and the *Pollux*'s death rattles. He listened harder. There it was again. Shouting. He raised his heavy head and tentatively shifted around to see what the fuss was about. Storekeeper Dupuy stood close to the edge of the rock, where Bettis had stood earlier, waving and shouting back and forth with the men clustered on the ship's railing. Carrying an extra 50 pounds in crude, he looked like a big, burnt black marshmallow, but there was no mistaking him. The guy was as loud as a foghorn.

The men at the ship's railing continued to wave and yell.

"We already tried to catch that line all morning," Califano grumbled.

Dupuy shouted back to them. "We tried ... didn't work."

When they persisted, Califano listened. He could hear snatches of their shouts: "cross ... main ledge ... catch ..."

They appeared to be set on having someone cross to the main ledge. To catch that line they were on about.

Dupuy decided to humour them. Califano watched as he made his way toward the narrow ridge connecting the rock that they were on to the main ledge. What was he thinking? A gully cut through that ridge. Califano rose to his knees to watch. Dupuy, barefoot, started to cross over. He checked out every slush hole and tested every slippery step, bending low to feel for cracks or juts of rock or ice that might give him a grip. Califano shook the fellows on either side of him. "Hey, boys, look. Dupuy's crossing to the main ledge."

The sailor on his left lifted his head slightly and lowered it again. The one on his right moaned, but didn't move.

Dupuy made it. Califano was impressed with his daring. Intermittent yells from the ship filtered through the clamour. Califano livened up. Finally, something was happening. A black object with a light line attached arced overhead and sailed straight for the ledge. Dupuy reached out and lost his balance. Califano froze. Roars erupted from the railing. Dupuy caught himself, straightened up, the light line in his hands. Crazed cheering cut through the gale.

Califano was on his feet. Bettis and a few others stirred at the commotion and roused up too. He and Bettis edged around the boys lying nearly comatose on the rock. Bettis crawled across first. Califano waited for him to reach the ledge, then he too crouched low and, on hands and knees, felt his way across the gap. Dupuy was already hauling in the 2-inch manila patched to the light line. There was blood on his hands, but Califano knew that he was long past feeling it.

Dupuy took a breather, looked back at the boys. "A drop of whiskey would come in handy, don't ya think?" he said, sporting a grin, lips cut and bleeding from the rope between his teeth. Tipping hand to mouth, he signalled the ship.

Califano chuckled. Even in these circumstances, Dupuy was a cocky bugger. Within minutes, a pint of Old Crow bobbed over the water. However, his grin died when his lifeless fingers were too numb to twist the cap. Refusing to relinquish it to Califano or Bettis, he tapped the neck on a rock.

"Careful," Califano cautioned. "You don't wanna croak with glass in your craw."

"You're right about that." Dupuy planted the bottle in a slushy dip and patted it with the heel of his hand. "For later." He continued to haul in the rope.

Califano and Bettis scanned the ledge for a sturdy spot to anchor the lifeline. There was none. Dupuy wasn't so fussy. Holding the rope between his teeth, on knees and elbows, he dragged himself to a rock protruding through a clump of ice and walked the line around it twice. Lying down, he wound the line snug around himself, planted his bare feet against the rock, and tugged it tight with his teeth and the flats of his hands. Califano and Bettis helped him secure it with five granny knots.

The bridge signalled that they'd pulled the line taut; it would hold.

Dupuy nodded his satisfaction, frostbitten claws tucked gingerly in his armpits. "Time for that drink, boys," he drawled. "Then we'll see about gettin' outta this hellhole."

Califano rescued the bottle. Dupuy raised it to his galled lips for the first taste.

▼▲▼

Joe Manning knew Lawn Head as well as any man.

He'd fished off there. He'd hunted ducks and turrs in the waters off Lawn Point and flushed out partridge on the barrens above. But neither man nor beast wanted to be caught near Lawn Head in a winter storm. He pondered what to do. Overnight, the first snow had blown in on an arctic gale. Lawn Head was only 4 miles by boat, but it was 10 or more miles of hard walking. Over rough country in the dirtiest weather, it would take up to five or six hours. And what if there was no foundation to the report? In Manning's mind, it might turn out to be a fool's errand. Besides, anyone still alive would be rescued by the time they reached Lawn Head. Still, if no one had got to them ... Maybe the horses could make it? The sleighs? Through thick woods with no trails to speak of?

Tom Connors and Jim Drake started off on foot to see if they could see a ship. Manning decided to go up on the ridge and have a gander. He harnessed the horse and sleigh and, just in case, gathered up a coil of new rope, two handlines, cod jiggers, an axe and started for the ridge with his son, Jim, and a neighbour, Fred Edwards, leaving half of Lawn praying for the poor souls who might be shipwrecked out there in this weather. The three drove to Three Stick Ridge. From there, they could see no sign of a ship. They carried on toward the coast to try and bring her into the open. And bring her open they did. She was like a big island.[96] Just like the boys had said. Manning stared at the ship. *If I was under that cliff, I'd like someone to come and try and save me.*

Heading back to the path, they met up with three more men who had also heard the news and decided to check it out. All hands agreed that there was nothing to do but go on to Lawn Head. Manning, having already eaten at noon, had no food for himself, or his horse. Alfred Grant had a small bite with him and some oats for his horse. Manning sent Jim home to look after his store. Fred was feeling poorly so he turned back as well, giving the two pieces of brown bread in his pocket to Manning. The others continued on. The rutted path—mainly a horse and ox track—was ice-covered in some places, buried under drifts in others. They wound around Little Lawn and climbed Breakheart Hill, picking up Drake and Connors along the way. Farther on, two more men with horses caught up with them.

Around 3 p.m., the group of eight men[97] and five horses veered off the path toward Lawn Head.

▼▲▼

Grindley lost no time in rigging a breeches buoy. He was assisted by Chief Gunner's Mate Jabin Berry, Shipfitter Bill Stanford, and a few other crewmen.

To test it, Turney sent across a load of heavy canned food and blankets. Not a hitch. Next, they needed a man over. Ensign Edgar Brown, a muscled tank of a fellow, easily 200 pounds and 6 feet tall, volunteered.

The *Pollux* signalled the men on the ledge. The crew quieted. They waited, dubious that the line would hold under Brown's substantial

---

96   Manning to Ryan, March 31, 1942.
97   According to both Rowsell and Brown, the men were Joe Manning, Jim Manning, Fred Edwards Alfred Grant, Tom Connors, James Drake, Robert Jarvis, Andrew Edwards, Martin Edwards, and Clarence Manning. Manning's letter, however, does not mention Clarence Manning.

brawn. If it slackened, Brown was in the drink. A dead man.

The line did threaten to founder as Brown closed in on the ledge. Grindley stood, rigid, until two sailors on the ledge inched forward and shouldered the line. Brown stepped out of the harness and saluted the ship. Chaos claimed the railing and turned the steeply canting deck into a brief wild shindig. While he waited for the breeches buoy to return for the next sailor, Grindley proved as good a back slapper as the next officer.

Aboard ship, spirits lifted. The officers supervised the evacuation. Each seaman carted his share of the supplies. Grindley ordered and double-checked that each sailor had secured a flashlight in his back pocket before stepping into the breeches buoy. He enforced it with repeated reminders. "It'll be dark before long. And we may have to walk a ways yet tonight."

As the crew waited their turn, they rooted for each mate in the harness until he landed on the ledge, while keeping a wary eye on the breeches buoy jouncing back to the ship. Then, with less than a dozen men across, the bulkhead forward of the engine room collapsed. Seas rushed in. The *Pollux* listed hard to starboard. The steep slant messed up evacuation royally. However, Grindley had considered that possibility and had more rope and an extra harness at the ready. He and the other officers managed to rig a second line from the flying bridge. Grindley and Bradley worked the lines, while Schmidt took charge of loading the men, one by one, into the harness. The officers strapped on their regulation .45 calibre pistols, Turney his sword.

Grindley, among the last remaining, collected his copious charts and workbooks. He would need them to answer to the Navy. He had seen this coming and had done everything in his power to steer them clear of Lawn Head. But eyeing the cumbersome stack, he decided that paperwork would not be his undoing. He left the pile in the doomed chart room and skimmed the wave-tops to the ledge. Stanford followed him. Then Berry. Turney, the last, stepped onto the ledge to shouts and salutes from his men. Grindley checked the time: 1630 hours. It would soon be dark. He did a quick count: 122 sailors were jammed on the ledge. Packed together like frozen fillets.

Twelve hours after running aground, the crew of the *Pollux* were delivered from the hell aboard ship—only to find themselves in limbo. Grindley cringed at the sight of the rock wall, browned by crude, looming over them. He joined a few of the more limber seamen checking the cliff for a way up. Having no success, he tried instead to gouge footholds in the sheet of ice. He got nowhere. They were up against time. As fast as the grey, winter daylight receded from Lawn Head, the tide rolled back in. It would, before long, overrun the ledge and every man on it. Anyone halfway alert darted glances to the overhang looming above them. Where were Garnaus, Greenfield, and DeRosa?

Where was the Navy?

▼▲▼

The cave staved off the wind and waves. But the heavily iced walls and the frozen ground the men flopped down on were enough to cause a man to wither.

Calemmo didn't mince words. "Shut your eyes here and you're a dead man," he warned, in a reasonable tone. If that didn't work, he notched it up, shouted at the fellow, hauled him to his feet if necessary, and sent him outside to check on the worsening state of the *Pollux*. Or the tide. Or the wind.

Gunner's Mate Wood attempted to fire his .45 automatic to get the *Pollux*'s attention; they didn't want to be forgotten here. But the mechanism was gummed up with crude. Next, he and a few others tried shouting, but there was no response from the ship. Wood pulled a Zippo lighter from an inside pocket and flicked it. To everyone's amazement, the Zippo worked. Wood managed to squeeze off a few sparks—enough to tease a meagre fire to life with junk they found scrounging the shingle. The mood brightened. A few started ripping apart lifejackets. The fibre stuffing caught, flickered, and burned. Calemmo hoped that they'd find enough wreckage on the beach to feed the greedy little blaze. Not for the heat—there was more smoke than flame.

But for the hope. It afforded them something to cling to.

▼▲▼

Dr. Bostic stepped onto the ledge cradling a 5-gallon can of medicinal alcohol. "Just a taste," he cautioned. "190 proof will burn your throat like battery acid."

Califano wet his lips, felt his tongue burn and then his throat, and passed the bottle. Grateful for the dry coat and shoes from the stores that the crew had brought across, he still couldn't quiet the shivering. Dr. Bostic enlisted the help of each new man on the ledge to look after the chilled sailors who had swum over. Califano watched as some of the boys were laid close together in a slight depression in the rock and covered with blankets and coats, awaiting rescue. He hoped that it wouldn't be a long wait.

As more and more men arrived, Califano was squeezed back into a nook at the base of the cliff. Although there was barely enough space to shift or shuffle, at least he was out of the drenching spray exploding over the ledge. The cleft, however, offered no protection from the penetrating, raw cold. After hours of exposure to extreme weather and seas, their chilled, sodden carcasses were badly equipped to generate heat, regardless of how close they were crammed together.

The worst, though, was underfoot. Sea water sloshed around their feet and shins. Numbness crept up their limbs. Califano recognized that the thread of hope keeping them alive was tenuous at best. He hoped that Calemmo and the men with him had found a way up the cliff and would send help. Squelching the niggling thought that they might have frozen to death, he jiggled to shake the feeling and generate body heat.

Anyone mobile moved: flexing fists, clapping hands, cupping ears, faces, bobbing up and down—any movement possible in tight quarters to keep the blood circulating and to hold numbness at bay. Next to Califano, Dupuy swore with gusto. Califano chuckled in spite of his misery. Dupuy still had the energy to get riled. Every time he shifted, one foot or the other slid down into a sinkhole until he was past his knees in slushy snow, with his feet slipping out of his shoes that had come across on the breeches buoy.

Pollack, fed up with lugging the moneybag padded in heavy Bunker C, pulled out a pocket knife and hacked off the cord that attached it to his belt. He set the bag in a hollow, all $47,000. "It ain't goin' nowhere," he growled, glaring at anyone who grinned. Califano looked up to the desolate rim of the cliff. Neither, it appeared, were they.

For a few minutes the boys had fun with Pollack. "We'll come to your court-martial, Paymaster," one of his mates ribbed. Another, through chattering teeth, added, "Hope your cell is warmer than this."

Frantic shouts shut them up. Necks craned. One sailor, close to the edge, lost his footing. Califano saw him slide. Wedged tight, he shouted, but couldn't get near the sailor. A buddy grabbed the sailor under the chin. But he too slipped. A third sailor gripped his legs. All three skidded toward the edge. Another sailor, aided by 100 hands and arms reaching, straining, clutched the legs of the third man. The first man slipped from his buddy's hands.

The ledge went deadly quiet.

▼▲▼

The going was hard, with each hill seemingly higher than the last.

With no trail to speak of, the Lawn men were up against stand of thick woods which they had to chop through. Then, assaulted by the cutting winds of the open barrens, they hunched together, backs to the whiteout. Mine Cove was barely visible in the distance. They pushed on, travelling parallel to the coast.[98] At Grebes Nest Pond, they stopped in a copse of scrub spruce to spell the horses, exhausted from breaking through the drifts. Manning figured that it was the first time that horses had ever gone from Lawn to Lawn Point. It was a difficult journey, without knowing if there would be anyone alive to save.[99]

A mile and a bit south of Grebes Nest Pond, they neared Big Hill. Manning made his way partway up the slope. Sure enough, there she was—ashore on Lawn Point, just outside of where Val Manning had his trap.[100] He shouted back to the others that there didn't seem to be a man alive. By the time he made it back down Big Hill, the others, except for Alfred, had gone ahead. Underfoot, it was one big sheet of glitter. They headed straight south to get there before dark; the light was already fading. When Manning and Alfred broke over the next hill, Bob came running back shouting, "Bring rope … there are bodies in the water."

Tom had gunned along this stretch of coast and knew the safest route down to the top of the cliff. Using their axes for purchase, they picked their way down the slope. In the twilight, not the might of the US Navy, but eight men from the small community of Lawn peered down the overhang. In the failing light, they made out a ship in deep distress, lying on her side, bleeding an oily scum that shrouded the shoreline and blackened the seas.

But the hardest to take in were the bodies; 50, 60, God knows how many were being thrown about in the water. The wind, whipping up and over Lawn Head, carried the sounds of slamming seas and the ship pounding on the rocks, but no sound or sign of life.

The men with horses needed to shelter them. A few hundred yards

98   Rowsell, *Waves of Courage*, 76.
99   Manning to Ryan, March 31, 1942.
100   Manning to Ryan, March 31, 1942.

inland, just below the brow of Lawn Head, there was a snag of stunted spruce in a hollow. "'Twill have to do," Manning said. Shortly after, axe in hand, intent on picking his way down back down to the rim, he met Tom calling for more rope as he scravelled back up.

Tom wheezed, "Survivors. Ashore on the rocks under the Head."

Under the Head? Then God help them.

▼▲▼

Seas spewing up the sides of the narrow gully cutting through the ridge knocked many men to their knees.

The overspill freshened the skein of ice underfoot. Grindley instructed the men to link arms. Strung along the pitted, slippery midline, they forged a chain of bodies braced against the barrage of tidewaters. Grindley kept a close eye on them.

Suddenly, James Hill, Seaman 1st Class, slipped and slid over the edge. Faster than the brain could process the horror. They heard his cries. Added their own. They saw his light blinking in the water. Then it was gone. To the last man, they would have given anything to save young Jimmy Hill. The men seemed to crumple. Grindley could see it in their faces and in the slump of their bodies. Up and down the line, the survivors clung to each other and prayed.

Night and the tide were closing in. The temperature had dropped further. Heavy spray saturated the crew. Strauss and a few cronies began to sing a popular World War I song, "There's a Long, Long Trail A-Winding." One by one, sailors added their voices. The soulful words echoed off the cliffs. On the outer edge of the ledge, Grayson, gazing up the cliff, sang his heart out: *"Old remembrances are thronging thro' my memory ..."*

"Look," he shouted, pointing up to the overhang. "It's Garnaus! He's back! With the Navy!"

▼▲▼

In the cove, Calemmo, Lloyd, and the 18 sailors stranded with them hugged close to the fire.

For a while, it provided a shred of cheer. But soon the ammo crates were gone, and then the kapok filling from their lifejackets. Calemmo sent anyone who could still haul himself to his feet to scrounge the shore for something to burn. The men returned with bits that could hardly be called chips.

Lloyd stood over them. Watching. The second an eye closed, he was on the fellow. "Hanson," he shouted. "What did I say? No sleeping. Outside. Go for a walk." Not content with Hanson's sluggish crawl, he grabbed his arm and dragged him outside. Seeing Mongeau lean back against the wall, he said, "You too, Mongeau. Hanson wants some company."

Calemmo roused the remaining men up, saying that it was time that everyone do a stay-alert march. "Except you, McCarron," he said. "You're the fire stoker for this watch."

"Aye, aye, sir," McCarron replied. "Bring back a cord of birch, will ya? Or maple?"

It took a while to get the lot of them on their feet; Calemmo and Lloyd ignored the groaning and mumbling. They knew that they should be moving about. But they no longer had the energy to care.

Darkness had fallen. Overhead, dark clouds raced across the sky, mostly obscuring the sliver of crescent moon. Eerie creaks and hisses from the *Pollux*, magnified in the dark, were unsettling. "What next?" Calemmo brooded. The tiny cove was as isolated as the grim coast. They were stuck in this crack in a wall of rock, in sub-zero temperatures, with no food, no survival gear, and no fire. And licking at their heels was a rising tide that would surely overrun the cove.

Calemmo wasn't a despairing man, but even he was hard-pressed to put a positive face on their circumstances.

▼▲▼

Above the ledge, the Navy had disappeared from sight.

Califano had barely seen them before they were gone. He blinked and rubbed his eyes. Looked again. Nothing. Either the welter of weather and darkening skies hid them, or his eyes had played a trick on him. Still, the others claimed they too had seen men up there. Anxious eyes strained up the cliff.

The officers, attempting to address their frustration, assured them that the Navy had the situation in hand. Mounting a rescue operation of this proportion, in these conditions, took considerable preparation and would be set in motion shortly, they reassured the men.

To Califano's mind, the officers didn't look as sure as they sounded.

While the crew waited for something to happen, they passed the time speculating how many Navy teams would have been deployed to the rescue effort. Someone added that a plane had flown over sometime in the afternoon, so there'd probably be assistance from Naval Aviation too. Others peered into the murk, looking for signs of US Navy warships. "They'd better send a fleet," someone said.

The rising tide menaced the ledge. Its reach, stretching higher and higher, smeared the rock with slick veneers of fresh ice.

Then retreated with the last of their supplies.

Still, neither Garnaus or the Navy reappeared on the clifftop.

▼▲▼

The Lawn men tramped back to the hollow. A place needed to be readied for the poor souls.

The gale blew up hard. The snow, blind-thick and drifting. Martin Edwards limbed branches from a dwarf spruce to make a bough shelter. Andrew set the spindly trunks aside to post a guideline up to the fire. On account of the bluff being cut by two deep gulches on both the east and west sides, they planted the scrawny posts in clumps of snow and strung a rope to lead the survivors up to the hollow and prevent their straying off toward the hazardous chasms. The cliff itself was also sloped back to a rocky gully. Manning and Grant scunned a second rope down that slope to aid the sailors in scaling the incline to the guideline.

They'd need a fire. Not an easy thing with boughs wet from everything being frosted over. Then Manning remembered that he had a few pieces of wood on the sleigh. Alfred shaved off some splits for kindling, chopped up the remaining boards, and struck a match. They stood around the blaze and planned how to bring the men up. All agreed that five men would be needed to hoist one sailor up the overhang. Alfred Grant said he'd be the front man; the others would line up behind him. The last man, the anchor, would wrap the rope around his waist for leverage.

"I think we're ready," Manning said. "Let's bring them up."

Standing in a swirl of snow and spray heaved up the cliff, they shone a light down to the ledge. Hands cupping mouths to save their words from the wind, they bellowed, "We'll haul you up. Shine your light so we can see you."

▼▲▼

A light flickered down the cliff.

A wind-muffled voice drifted down the overhang.

"We can't get you up from where you are." There was a pause.

"You'll have to come over here." Another pause.

"One man at a time."

"Commander," Grindley said, on the quiet, "the voice is coming from the overhang above the ledge."

Turney's nod was slight. He beamed his emergency lamp up the cliff.

Grindley had checked out that narrow ridge of rock when he'd first arrived on the ledge. It was pure treachery underfoot. The men would have to jump across the hazardous gully that cut through it. Black water sluiced up the sides, growing wilder with the running tide. Grindley's insides tightened. God forbid that anyone misstep.

Stanford, closest to the ridge, jumped across the gully and positioned himself below the voices. He stuck his flashlight in the slush, angling it as best he could to light the ridge. He called up to the men on the overhang, "We're ready."

Grindley sucked back a breath. There was no room for a false step.

"The worst off will be sent up first," Turney directed, "and then those less disabled. The remaining crew will go according to their position on the ledge."

The officers lined the men along the ledge and stationed themselves down the line to shield them as much as possible from the tide hurtling up the gully. Grindley and Grayson beamed their lights along the ridge.

"It's tight," Stanford yelled. "Only a couple at a time."

The first sailor, head bandaged and limping badly, was helped over the gully. Stanford secured the rope around his chest. Though the darkness made for limited visibility, all eyes were glued to the sagging body inching upward in starts and stops. Then the next man. And the next.

Pollack was sent up because of his badly skinned right leg, caught between the raft and the hull when he and Boundy had climbed the cargo net after being thrown out of the raft. The money bag and briefcase went with him. When the last of the injured were hoisted up, Dr. Bostic followed, clutching his can of medicinal alcohol. Next, a mishmash of clothing was sent up, including boots, shoes, and blankets.

The officers also sent Dupuy up early; he'd done his duty. His shoes had been left behind in the sinkhole. Next they decided to send up a sailor in relatively good health to help out. Grindley surveyed the crew, most of them in rough shape. Toward the back, he spotted George Coleman, Boatswain's Mate 2c Class, bobbing and dancing to keep life in his limbs. Grindley summoned him. Hand to hand, his mates edged him forward.

Satisfied that Coleman was in better shape than most, Grindley sent him across with an order. "You're to assist at the top any way you can."

Coleman bobbed his head. "Yes, sir. I will, sir."

Grindley beckoned to the next in line. The sailor jumped the gap and made it. Then, without warning, two anxious sailors jumped at the same time. Grindley shouted, but it was too late. The two smacked into one another and fell forward into the gully. Cries of raw anguish went up. In a flash, Bradley threw himself across the gap, grabbing the other side to block the men from being washed out to sea. He was too late; the men were already gone. Stanford and another sailor hauled Bradley back. Blood spurted from a deep gash in his arm. They applied a tourniquet above his elbow and sent him up to Dr. Bostic.

"Can you move the operation along faster?" Grindley shouted across the gap to Stanford.

"We have to wait for the okay from above," Stanford hollered back.

Turney swung his lamp back and forth, rallying his crew into mustering their last reserves. He urged them to stay alert, to hang on to each other. "We made it this far," he said. "If we stand together, we can make it up the cliff too."

Minutes later, Grindley started as a wave knocked Chief Pharmacist's Mate O'Connor head over heels. Retired from the Navy, he had been recalled in 1939 to serve aboard the *Pollux*. Thankfully, Strauss grabbed O'Connor and shielded him with his body. The man lay there stunned. Grindley elbowed a way through to him. "Help him over to Stanford," he directed Strauss. O'Connor was next to go up; then Strauss.

At least there was no wind on the ledge; the crew were somewhat sheltered between the ship and the cliff. The tide, however, continued to rise.

Heavy seas rammed through the gully. Reached for the remaining men. Tore at them. Picked them off one by one—the young and inexperienced, the old, the careless. For the rest, the waves broke first their bodies and then their spirits. The officers kept close watch on the men kneeling in the slush, on the sailor snaking slowly up the overhang, and on the time.

Lieutenant Paul Weintraub checked his watch. Full tide, at roughly 2230 hours, was only an hour away. In an aside to Grindley, he said, "We're nearing peak tide. Conditions could worsen yet."

Grindley's nod was terse. A youngster, overhearing them, blanched in fear.

"Steady, sailor," Grindley reassured him. "We're almost there."

He hoped to God it was so.

▼▲▼

In the cove, the hours wore on. The fire was mere cinders and ash.

Someone mumbled, "Oil everywhere, and not even a twig to burn." The sailor next to him pulled a clump of crude from the sleeve of his jacket and flung it on the ashes. There was a small burst of flame. The others did the same. The flare-ups, however, lasted only as long as the time it took to throw the gobs.

Then a young sailor, lying lifeless in a drift of snow, suddenly roused up, shouting and raving. Before Calemmo, or Lloyd, or anyone else could move to stop him, he lunged toward the embers and doused the last few sparks with his bare hands. The men went berserk. Tore into the sailor. Wood even pulled out his useless gun. But the sailor had already fallen. He lay in the ashes. Insensible.

Calemmo talked the men down. They knew that the fellow was not in his right mind, but it was difficult not to lash out. Calemmo understood. He felt the plunge into darkness as keenly as the others. The last of their hope died along with those meagre embers.

No one spoke the words, but all recognized that they couldn't last much longer.

▼▲▼

On the ledge, the night progressively worsened. If that was possible.

The seas had stolen the last of their stash of clothing and food. Califano watched a heavy carton of canned goods shift sideways from the middle of the ledge. Seconds later, it was picked up and lobbed over the edge. The ship's records, secured in tarps and raincoats, were long gone too. Through it all, the grating and thudding of the broken *Pollux* was an excruciating constant.

Sailors with flashlights had switched them on and shoved them in their back pockets. There was still a line of men ahead of Califano. He patiently waited his turn; some men on the ledge were in worse shape than he. In the faint beam of lights, his gaze drifted to the overhang. What was up there? And who? With waters too rough for a Navy hospital ship to assist, had the brass set up a field hospital? Or, maybe there was a town nearby with a hospital? And a warming centre? He hoped so. Unable to withstand the steadily increasing force of waves tearing through the gully and rushing the ledge, his legs buckled. Others lay prostrate in an attempt to resist the surf's drag.

When they had first arrived on the ledge, Califano had heard the officers say that the count was about 122 men. Four had already been taken by the seas. Then Ensign Xavier Clarke,[101] fresh out of Harvard, was lifted up and carried off on a monster of a wave, the only sign of his death a keening on the wind. The surviving seamen clung to each other in the cramped space, the officers as speechless, as undone, as their ratings.

Califano knelt in the slush. Shaken. Finally, his turn came. He was hoisted up the cliff, too terrified to open his eyes. Swinging above the

---

101   The only officer on the *Pollux* to lose his life.

crazed North Atlantic, the rough rope digging sharply into his chest and flesh of his underarms, he skirted the edge of panic. His temple grazing the icy cliff face smartened him up, and he opened his eyes. Unable to see a thing in the black night, and afraid to look down, or up, he reached out, and touching the rock wall, used his frozen fists and feet to guide himself up the cliff. Voices alerted him he was nearing the top. Gentle. Assuring.

"We got you, sonny ... take it easy now ... let us do the work."

Califano glimpsed shadows of men on their knees at the edge of the cliff. Arms reached for him, drew him closer, latched on to the rope around his chest and pulled him over the brink. He lay there, catching his breath, feeling the solid frozen ground under him. Getting to his feet to thank his rescuers, the wind on the scarp knifed through him—a caution the night wasn't yet done with the *Pollux* and her crew.

Someone—he wasn't alert enough to realize that it wasn't the Navy—grabbed his arm and guided him, staggering down a slope that was as rocky as his legs were rubbery. He was then led up the other side, where he was passed off to someone else. That someone knew his name, called him Ernie. Califano squinted through the weather. "Coleman, is that you?"

"Nah, I'm your guardian angel," Coleman quipped, hurrying him uphill through a snowdrift.

"Where the hell are we?"

Coleman laid Califano's hand on the guideline, taking steady breaths between each word. "Uphill ... a half-mile ... there's a fire and shelter. Can you make it on your own?"

Califano nodded, stopping to catch his breath. "Is there something to eat up there?"

Coleman turned to go back. "Don't let go of the line," he warned. "There's chasms on either side ... ya hear?"

Califano rubbed his dud leg. "What about coffee? Any coffee?"

But Coleman was stuck on the one track. "Don't let go of the line."

"Aye aye, sir," Califano replied, without saluting. There'd better be coffee. He stumbled headlong up the slope, eyes burning and tearing from oil fumes, the head-to-toe shakes beyond his control. The intense throbbing in his good foot caused him to flinch at every clumsy step; the other foot, a dead thing he dragged behind him.

Without warning, the line ended. Some guideline they'd rigged, he thought. There was no post in the snow either. And not a glimmer of light anywhere. Where was he? Where was the fire Coleman promised? And the shelter? Unable to see, unable to hear anything but galing winds and the drumming of the *Pollux*'s hull on the rocks, Califano was in a pickle. He floundered about and fell. His hand landed on a pack of Pall Malls—a gift from God! He sat up, felt around for matches, vowing, "I'm havin' a smoke if it's the last thing I do."

Not a single strike. In either pocket. A pack of Pall Malls in his mitt and no light! This surely was a cursed night. He hollered into the black, "Help! ... Help! ... Dupuy? ... Anybody?" Good thing he did yell. Someone showed up and dragged him to the hollow, the Pall Malls clutched in his frozen paw.

He was drained from the effort of that half-mile hike, uphill all the way. Wincing in pain, he slumped down by a fire that was a few licks of flame and the rest smoke.

He thought for sure there'd be something to eat. Or drink.

▼▲▼

The young sailor the officers had sent up to help was a godsend—freeing Manning to spell as the outside man on the rope.

Coleman appeared to be none the worse for the hardship he had come through. Two shoes on his feet and not a graze on him. Back and forth he went, lugging the men to the handline traversing the gully, up the steep, rocky slope another hundred yards to the guideline. From there, it was another hefty hike, uphill a half-mile or more, to the hollow.

On the rope, the hands of the five men were welted and blistered. Backs aching, knees almost buckling under the weight, and arms feeling like they were being ripped out of their sockets, they persevered, pausing only for the time it took to change positions on the rope—in case a different bearing might ease the burden.

They ran a loose tally: 20 men up, then 35.

Bulked up and blackened with crude, they could hardly be recognized as human. Almost half the crew had been brought up, according to a survivor just off the rope. Back and forth, up and down the incline, Coleman dragged his shipmates until he himself was ready to drop. Seeing as more survivors were coming to the aid of their shipmates, one of the men told him to take a break by the fire; after, he returned halfway to pick up sailors handed off by mates who waited at the rim.

However, there was no let-up for the men on the rope. Sixty or so survivors had been hauled up. Each man arriving at the top told of the desperate circumstances below: several of the crew had washed overboard, waves were rushing the gully, the tide was fast reaching the top of the ledge, threatening more lives—and begging them to hurry. Then, with about 30 men still on the ledge, reinforcements arrived. And none too soon, as far as the worn-out Lawn men were concerned. Ready to drop, they gratefully handed over the rope to the St. Lawrence miners Henry Lambert, Patrick Tarrant, Alfred Turpin, and Mick Turpin and his brother, Pius Turpin.

"You fellas are a welcome sight," Manning declared.

"Amen to that," seconded Alfred.

Stanford tugged on the rope and the last of the *Pollux*'s crew swayed ponderously up the scarp.

Grindley felt enormous relief. Stanford had been a titan through the whole ordeal, standing on the exposed ridge for hours. With only a few officers and Turney left, he insisted on finishing the job. Secured around the chest, Weintraub noted the time: 2330 hours. "Against the deadliest odds, we've survived high tide," he commented.

Grindley flinched at his words. The four crewmen snatched from the ledge hadn't made it. Nor had young Ensign Clarke.

Weintraub was followed soon after by Grayson. Only Turney, Grindley, and Stanford remained. Turney stood firm. He would go last. Stanford agreed on the condition that the commander practice the proper knot on him until he was satisfied that he had it right. Turney nodded assent. Stanford tied Grindley to the rope. The two shook hands.

Grindley struggled to keep an even voice. "See you at the top, my friend."

Stanford saluted him, tugged, and the rope edged upward. Grindley guided himself along the jutting clumps of ice, wondering how the injured and sick had managed to fare. It would not have been an easy ascent for any of them, but especially so for the infirm. Surely, by now they were safe and being cared for.

He reached the overhang unscathed, allowed himself to be helped over the edge to safety, and finding his feet, slid out of the rope without assistance—keen to take the measure of the scene before him. In the dim beam of a propped-up flashlight, his eyes raked over the cramped circle—the few men, the dirty, trodden snow, smears of blood. And nothing else.

Grindley and the other officers watched, transfixed, as five men ground the heels of their rubber boots into gravel and ice to purchase a secure grip. Wrapping welted hands around the rope, their five energies fused as one, laboured to bring Turney, a stout fellow, up the cliff. Their drive to secure this last man was as single-minded as a father's to save his son. The toll evident in the strain on their weary faces, on their bowed backs.

Those few men, ill-equipped and physically exhausted, had done this for 120 sailors? His brain screamed, Where is the Navy? Grindley didn't hang around for the commander to set foot on the bluff.

Close to 0030 hours, he set off up the gully to the guideline, and on toward shelter.

▼▲▼

Unable to make contact with the *Pollux*, Calemmo, Lloyd, and their 18 shipmates waited.

They were still unaware of the whereabouts of Garnaus, Greenfield, and DeRosa. Calemmo and Lloyd had tried all day to keep the men awake. Lloyd barked at McCarron, who had begun to doze. McCarron gave a start and opened his eyes, complaining that he was parched. He turned and licked the icy rock wall. From time to time, he turned back to the wall for another lick. It helped keep him awake, he said, but left him even thirstier.

With the little fire dead and the night's cold bearing down, the will of the small band of survivors died too. Foster[102] curled up, head on his knees. No amount of shouting roused him. Jewett, too, had gone silent. Nudged by the fellow next to him, he fell over. As did Mongeau, Hanson, Storekeeper Hak, and Mess Attendant Tommie Harris. The men, unresponsive, had given up.

Unable to beat back the dark, the cold, the pain, they were freezing to death.

Separated from one another, each hunched-over man isolated in a

---

102   Phillips's friend, Mess Attendant 3rd Class James Foster, did not survive.

cold, black hole of nothingness, it was too easy to sink deeper into the well of darkness. As much the mind's doing as the body's. The evening dragged on. Then the night.

Four others lost the fight to stay awake.

▼▲▼

Somewhere between the ledge and the hollow, Califano had lost his other shoe.

In no time, his eyes went from blurry to blind, first from the crude and then the smoky fire.

Dr. Bostic had run out of medicinal alcohol. Nicosia, having managed to bring a few bottles of his personal stash of whiskey, rationed it out to the worst off. Califano, apparently, wasn't one of them. Anyone half alive had no chance of a sniff, let alone a taste of the liquid gold.

Brown and the doctor harangued the men to stay on their feet, to keep moving. Dr. Bostic told anyone who would listen that he thought that their best bet was to walk to town. "At least you won't be falling asleep."

Pollack mulled it over. Wearing his swim trunks, boots, and his goon jacket, he said he couldn't feel a thing. Not even his bad leg. "Must be the grease." He called out to Dr. Bostic. "Where is this place? Do you think we can find our way in the dark?"

"Follow the shore," Dr. Bostic said. "You're bound to come to it. Sooner or later."

Pollack and Bollinger, figuring they were better off on the move, decided to go. Four or five others agreed and gathered around them. Dupuy, being who he was, wanted to go but decided against it: he had no shoes. Califano wished he could join them, but his shoeless and half-blind state kiboshed any hope of that. The crew wished them good luck. Califano hobbled around the fire with the others, careful to follow behind someone at the outer ring. "Where's Larry?" Califano asked. "Is he up from the cove yet?"

"Not yet," Brown replied, preoccupied with the men around the fire. He ordered the more able ones down the hill to help their shipmates just off the rope to negotiate the trail up to the hollow.

The Navy finally had arrived, someone said. A handful. Overland. With some blankets and a few cans of soup and juice that had frozen on the way. By the time Califano got wind of it, the blankets and the rations were already meted out. A few locals straggled in from over the hills. He missed out too on the few slices of bread they handed out— gone before he could get to it.

In between griping about the Navy, they called out their mates' names, hoping to hear them respond. Over and over, shipmates pestered Dr. Bostic and Brown, asking after mates. "What about Mongeau? How about Jewett ... anyone seen Jewett?"

On Califano's mind was his buddy. "Where's Calemmo? Is he up yet?"

▼▲▼

The Lawn men made their way to the hollow. It was a godforsaken sight.

They were prepared for the feeble state of the sailors, but seeing them all together—bowed double from the harsh wind and merciless cold, lying lifeless on the frozen ground at the edge of the bit of fire, or dragging their shipmates around it—the enormity of the tragedy hit them. So many were pressing in toward the feeble flames, their rescuers had to throw boughs up and over the men's heads to reach the fire. The best they could do until more help arrived was to try and keep them alive.

Stunted growth along the coast never really dried out. In any season. The frozen boughs cranked out clouds of smoke—and were noisy with sizzle and spit, not the crackle of heat. The rescuers, themselves exhausted, having had neither food nor rest in over 12 hours, were forced to range farther out in search of firewood.

The US Navy had arrived sometime during the evening. Not like you would expect. Just small groups of them. In dribs and drabs, three or four at a time. From ships docked in St. Lawrence harbour, they said. They scoured the slope for wood alongside the Lawn men, hefting back to the hollow armfuls of small trees, which the sailors referred to as Christmas trees.

Miners from Iron Springs and Director Mines arrived around the same time and joined the effort—many of the same men who had rescued the crew of the *Truxtun*. Scouring the hillside for firewood, a few thought that they heard someone calling out and shinnied down the slope for a closer look. A local man also thought that he'd heard voices calling for help, and joined them. From the rim of the cove, their flashlights played over the rocks below. There was no response to their calls.

"At first light, we'll come back for a good look," said one of the Lawn men.

Agreeing, the group made their way back to the fire.

The hollow looked like a clear-cut.

A thick bank of black smoke roofed the whole depression. Heavy fog leaned on everything. A fire, small by any standard, flickered in the basin of the hollow. With every armload of wet boughs, it belched more smoke, choking out most of the flames. In these conditions, the wonder was that the rescuers had managed to keep a fire burning at all. With nowhere to go, the smoke hung suspended in the air, burning oil-crudded eyes and irritating the noses and throats of the men tottering around it.

Grindley checked the perimeter. Many sailors lay dead. Others, incoherent, raving, were more dead than alive. Like himself, the whole lot of them had nothing in their stomachs, not having eaten since the ship ran aground 24 hours ago, and now that they were on solid ground, they were beginning to feel it.

Grindley spotted Navy corpsmen issuing medicinal alcohol to the survivors, and to those in poor condition, injections of stimulants. Grayson informed Grindley that the corpsmen had come by float plane from Argentia and had walked overland from town. Another group of a half-dozen or so Navy personnel from the *Badger* and the *Brant* had gone to gather firewood. Grayson added that the ships had left the Argentia Naval Base at 0800 hours for the eight-hour passage across Placentia Bay. Before departure, they had discussed the matter of food and clothing for the survivors but decided that since the *Pollux* was a supply ship, that would not be a concern. They carried only limited medical supplies that were standard equipment for any rescue needs.[103]

Grindley spat his reply. "There's nothing standard about this rescue mission, Ensign. It's nothing short of an unmitigated tragedy."

With that, he swallowed his anger and continued on a round of the circle. Earlier, he had watched Dupuy set a can of snow close to the fire. As he was about to pull back the blackened can of melted snow, a fellow who could barely stand scuffed by, knocking it over. "Nooooo," Dupuy groaned, crawling back to his blanket. Grindley refilled the can for him and set it close enough to the fire that it was practically in the flames.

Brown, constantly checking on the men, insisted that they stay awake and keep moving. Grindley admired his persistence, his devotion to the men in his charge. In spite of his frostbitten face and hands, the junior officer had been keeping vigil on the surviving crew since the first ones were brought up hours ago.

Bradley was a cause for concern. Dr. Bostic had rigged up a makeshift sling and tied him to a scrawny tree to keep him from keeling

---

103   Brown, *Standing into Danger*, 223.

over. A corpsman had given him a shot, Dr. Bostic said. Grindley kept going back to check on him.

With all the crew up the cliff, the number of men around the fire had grown so large that there was barely space to move. Grindley spotted an oily life jacket, assigned a junior the job of ripping it apart, and started another little fire just beyond the edge of the circle of men by firing a still-functioning flare gun into it. The brief flare-ups caught the attention of others, who wandered over. A few fellows went to work tearing up their own life jackets to feed the mingy flames. Grindley wondered if that was wise. The sodden life jackets provided more warmth on the body than the scrawny fire. He said nothing. The effort gave them something to do and kept them awake.

Grindley kept track of Strauss, who was showing signs of being slightly delirious from sleep deprivation. When he was nowhere to be seen, Grindley went looking and found him asleep. He hauled Strauss to his feet, shook him, and slapped his face to bring him around. But, close to dawn, Grindley too nodded off. Catching himself, he jumped up and, realizing that Strauss was missing again, he went in search of him. Luckily, he heard a voice calling for Jo—the name of Strauss's girlfriend. He found Strauss on his knees in a snowdrift and helped him back to the fire, giving him a good tongue-lashing along the way. Strauss stayed awake after that.

Shortly after, a small party of locals arrived in the hollow by foot. After distributing crackers and a few bits of bread, they tended to the survivors—walking some around the fire, massaging the limbs of others. Still others searched the hillside for something more to burn. Grindley joined them. He recognized one of them as one of the men who had worked the rope, the anchorman, heading uphill with an armload of boughs. "When do we move out?" Grindley asked.

The man paused. "At daybreak." Soft spoken, not given to idle talk, he shifted his load. "More help on the way."

Grindley nodded. "I'll take that off your hands."

The man bobbed his head, lowered the bundle, and turned to go back down the hill for another load of wood.

Grindley shouldered the boughs and made his way up the hill, preoccupied with the compromised state of many of the crew, particularly those who had swum ashore. Besides the physical trauma they had endured, for hours now they had now been in wet clothing in sub-zero temperatures and a raging gale. He, in dry gear, felt his legs and hands numbing. How in God's name were they enduring? He feared for them.

They may have survived the destruction of the *Pollux*. But would they—could they—survive the rescue?

▼▲▼

In the cave, one man after another lowered head to knees and drifted off.

Calemmo and Lloyd gave up shouting at them. They no longer had the energy or the desire to stay awake.

Lloyd turned and put his hand on Calemmo's shoulder. "I guess this is the end, buddy," he said. "It looks like we're not going to make it." He lowered his head, a hand still on Calemmo's shoulder.

Calemmo nodded slightly, "I guess you're right, Lloyd," he responded, in a hoarse whisper. "Good luck, my friend." Arms resting on drawn-up knees, Calemmo lowered his head to rest on his arms. He closed his eyes.

The clatter of falling rock brought him back. Too sluggish for movement, he managed to raise his head. Through slitted eyes he spied, in the mouth of the cave, lights and vague shadows. He wasn't sure he could trust his senses . . . But the shower of scree and ice was real. And the voice that called out had an earthy accent. Calemmo flailed about until he got his legs working.

He stumbled toward the lights, with Lloyd close on his heels.

Califano roused up. "Where's Larry?"

No one answered, each man deep in his own affliction. Califano had dropped to the ground to rest for a spell, at a reasonable distance from the fire. Some had edged awfully close to the flames. Brown, on his rounds, kept nudging them back. A fellow with frozen limbs had to be careful. Without knowing, he could scorch a hand or foot. Califano roused up again, and like a stuck record, repeated. "Is Larry up yet?"

Brown shook his head, "Not yet. But it's high time we find them and bring them up." Califano could see that Brown was nearing the end of his patience. "They should have been rescued hours ago along with the rest of the crew," Brown muttered.

Unaware that a party had already scouted the area above the cave, he tried to scrounge up a few men to make the trek down the hill in search of Calemmo, Lloyd, and the others the seas had taken into the cove. It was a tough sell, with the survivors themselves barely hanging on, but Brown, bent on cobbling together a rescue party, continued to nag them. Califano was right behind him. Brown laid into the boys, "Those men are your shipmates. Are you just going to leave them stranded in the cove?"

Overhearing Brown, one of the Lawn men asked, "Did you say there were men still below?"

"Trapped in the cove," Brown replied.

Without a word, they headed down the hill. Trailing after them, some of the sailors Brown had worked on all night.

Califano sank back down on the ground.

He shut his burning eyes. And waited.

▼▲▼

Fishermen turned hard-rock miners, eking out a hand-to-mouth existence on the edge of the North Atlantic, the Newfoundlanders knew tragedy up close.

But the sight they laid eyes on, as they trained their lights on the black maw of that cranny, was a shock even to them. An oily ring of black humps, half buried in drifts, filled the crevice and slumped toward the remains of a fire. Others leaned off to the side. There was no sign of life. Nothing even to indicate that these were men and not wreckage—until the lantern beam picked up a logy stir from one lump and then a single, squinched-up eye.

Roused by the racket, the sluggish pile of crude shifted and separated. Heads, arms, legs emerged from the heap as a dozen or more men staggered or crawled toward the lights and voices.

The Newfoundlanders, heartened that the sailors were still alive, spared no time for talk. The first man was roped around the chest and sent topside. On its return, the rope had barely hit the shingle when the next man was sent up the cliff. Those showing no signs of life, they left until last.

At the top, the Lawn men waited along with a few Navy rescuers and a handful of shipmates sent by Brown to assist. They eased the sailors, one after another, from the rope. Some were barefoot, others without jackets, their shirts and dungarees stiffened with frost. The notion of tackling those hills, the shrieking wind slashing right to the bone, the cold even more brutal than below, was more than enough to cause a body to crumple to the ground. Their shipmates allowed the rescued men scant time to dwell on it. Two men took each sailor by the arms, and dragged him up the endless rise, coaxing him with the promise of a fire. The poor fellows squinted at desolate hills laced with snow and ice, and shut their bleary eyes in despair.

Alfred Grant noted the dry gear of the Navy rescuers and enlisted their assistance with the sailors who hadn't made it.

▼▲▼

Calemmo, Lloyd, and the others who had been stranded in the cove arrived in the hollow.

Grindley noted the time: 0450 hours.

With each new arrival, their shipmates crowded around to see who had survived. The newly rescued sailors, oblivious to the attention, buckled in defeat at the sight of the hollow's poor excuse for rescue and shelter.

Grindley recognized Apprentice Seaman Brewer who came from the South, and told him to lie in the snow to ward off the shrill wind. Stupefied, Brewer did. Dr. Bostic jabbed him with a needle. Grindley tied a piece of torn blanket around his swollen foot and kept an eye on him. Officers directed a few others to lie in the snow as well. Grindley, heart ripped out of his chest, packed more snow around them and assured them that they would be leaving shortly.

Calemmo was the last to arrive at the hollow under his own steam, shoeless, but lucid. Brown steered him toward Califano. Calemmo dropped at the edge of the puny flames next to his pal.

"Not much of a welcome party," Calemmo grumbled, falling against Califano.

Califano shoved him back and made a feeble attempt to grab him in a headlock.

"Hey, buddy, what took you so long? We're all out of coffee and smokes."

But Calemmo was already dead-to-the-world asleep, head heavy on Califano's shoulder.

Grindley marvelled at their spunk. In spite of what they'd been through, these two would make it. He cracked a slight smile and moved on.

McCarron, as full of blarney as ever, said he'd come 'round roped around the chest, halfway up the cliff. He didn't know, at first, if he was dead or alive. Two sailors towed him up to the shelter, threw a blanket over his shoulders, and lowered him down by the little fire. McCarron's pal, Pete Manger, lay on the ground beside him.

"Hey, Pete," he rasped.

"Pete didn't make it," someone said.

McCarron was at a loss for words. For the longest time, he didn't move. He sat on the ground next to Manger, knees up to his chin, one hand covering his eyes, the other resting on his buddy's shoulder.

Others from the cove were delivered to the hollow unconscious. On stretchers contrived from blankets. With ferocious zeal, Dr. Bostic, Dr. Longnecker (who'd arrived with the Navy dispatch), and several corpsmen massaged their limbs. In time, Hanson and Mongeau came around. Harris did not respond. Hak died shortly, his head cradled in Dupuy's lap.

Dupuy covered him with his own blanket.

Grindley scanned the hills for the promised "help on the way."

▼▲▼

First light.

Darkness surrendered its hold on Lawn Head. Gradually. Reluctantly. Damage done, it slunk away. Clouds retreated. Fog eased off, straggly shreds trailing across the barrens. The Lawn men, chilled to the marrow, and as famished and fatigued as the men they'd rescued, decided it was best that they head out. Iron Springs was a three-hour walk. The distance to Lawn was more than twice that. They harnessed the five horses to sleighs ready to transport as many men as they could to Iron Springs.

Turney tasked Dr. Bostic with the difficult decision of who should go first. The doctor, squinting through bloodshot eyes, regarded the worst-off of his charges: Jewett and Hanson, who had been trapped in the cave; Bradley, because of the alarming gash in his arm; and Dupuy, due to his dangerously frostbitten hands and feet, were among those who received the nod.

With an injured man secured to each sleigh (two on Manning's), the Lawn men set out for Iron Springs, leaving their axes behind for others to keep the fire going. They didn't know the country from Lawn Head to St. Lawrence. With no trail to speak of (and no axes with which to cut one), the going was tricky. Ten minutes in, one of the survivors asked if it was much farther. Manning felt for him; he hoped the poor youngster would pull through.

For close to three hours, they lumbered uphill and down, coaxing the horses through drifts and across stretches of ice, straining to keep the sleighs upright and steady on the rough terrain so as not to further injure the ailing sailors, and heaving all their weight against them when they tilted and threatened to overturn on a hillside.

None too soon, Alfred spotted a light in the distance. Manning nodded.

The headframe of Iron Springs.

▼▲▼

The remaining survivors sensed a shift in their situation and rallied. Well over 100 sailors awaited rescue.

Turney and his officers decided to take advantage of the crew's renewed energy. Those able to walk would start out on foot, in groups, with a St. Lawrence man in the lead.

Then someone circling the fire spied a crowd on the crest of a hill a ways off and shouted, "It's the Navy! The rescue party is here."

There were no hurrahs. Most didn't have the energy to even look up. Closer, the crowd separated out to be local men herding horses, oxen, and even dogs harnessed to sleds. Food was foremost on every survivor's mind. But the group that traipsed into the hollow, having emptied their shops and pantries for the *Truxtun* rescue effort, toted only crackers and a few tins of soup that turned out to be frozen.

Grindley assigned Calemmo and Califano to Henry Lambert's group. "He'll look out for you."

The wiry Newfoundlander took the lead. "Keep your hand on the shoulder of the man in front of you," he said in a lilting brogue, "and you'll be okay. If you fall, the man behind you is to call out." He paused and eyed them shyly. "Don't dwell on it now. You'll make it ... I promise you that."

The men nodded, grateful for the assurance from this kind stranger. Calemmo edged into line behind Califano. "As long as there's coffee when we get there," he said. "And food."

Before starting off, Henry stuck Calemmo's bare feet into boots. "They're two lefties," he said. "But better than none." Left or right, Calemmo didn't object. He couldn't feel a thing anyway.

A young American coast guardsman, bringing up the rear, disappeared and returned minutes later with a pair of rubber boots for Califano; the boots were several sizes too big; Califano wore them anyway.

"Aren't we characters?"

Calemmo replied, "Yeah, cartoon characters."

Henry's group started off in the dim light of early morning. They were barely out of sight of the hollow when Brewer fell behind. The rag bandaging his foot had come off in a drift. He tried to keep up until his other sock and shoe were gone too. The coast guardsman called a halt. He tried to give Brewer his arctic boots; they wouldn't fit over Brewer's swollen feet. He offered his pea jacket; it wouldn't fit Brewer's 6-foot frame. The group plodded along. The wind had abated, the snow had stopped, the sky was getting lighter. Califano, sinking thigh-deep in drifted-in hollows, was hauled out by Calemmo; Califano returned the favour on the next drift.

Nicosia tramped up and down the line, reviving the abject little band with "just a taste now" of his all-but-empty, last bottle of whiskey.

Eventually, they came to Chambers Cove and then the tilt at the bottom of the ravine. Sliding down, they practically ran into a man with a horse and sleigh. The American coast guardsman loaded Brewer on, his big, black feet stretched out on a plank in front of him. Off they went, the Newfoundlander walking alongside his horse, Maude, sweet-talking it into tackling the next hill.

Henry and the coast guardsman similarly coaxed the men through another hour of what seemed like the back end of hell as one sailor, then a second man, and a third crumpled in the snow. "We're close enough," Henry said. He lugged them to a shelter of a stand of fir trees. "Wait here," he said. "I'm going to the mine for a truck. I won't be long."

A truck? Calemmo eyed the open barrens. He couldn't see a road, but with the sorry state of his eyes, he wasn't about to argue the point. He, Califano, and a few others sank to the ground to wait. Califano's eyes were still sore but, away from the smoke, had begun to clear.

The coast guardsman waited with them while Henry set out, with a few others, for the mine. "It's not far now," he told them. "Less than half a mile."

Within a short time, Calemmo and Califano heard the roar of a truck. Still, it was long enough for one of the young recruits to get his hand, clamped around a sapling, frozen stuck. They couldn't prise it loose, so Henry cut down the sapling with his pocket knife and put the fellow and the tree in the cab.

Calemmo climbed into the back of the truck and pulled Califano after him.

"This is more like it," Califano pronounced.

They bounced over ruts and drifts right up to the door of the mine house. Henry jumped out of the cab and extracted the young sailor, still clenching the sapling. Califano patted his shoulder.

"Hey, buddy," he said, "Looks like you got attached to that little Christmas tree … you bringin' it home for a souvenir?"

The junior managed a dull grin. Calemmo, Califano, and the others traipsed inside the mine house.

After that, Califano and Calemmo lost track of each other. Someone took Califano away to attend to his eyes. He was fed a bowl of soup before he boarded a truck for the short ride to the *Badger* docked in the harbour. Calemmo was taken to a pile of clothes. He was stripped— so fast he didn't have time to be embarrassed—and dressed in dry dungarees and a shirt. He kept his two left boots. The only coat that came anywhere near to fitting him was a captain's blue uniform jacket, brass buttons and all. Calemmo baulked. He'd be court-martialled if he tried to board the *Brant* wearing that! But wear it he did; there was nothing else that fit him. He spent the rest of the day cringing and blurting his fireman's rank every time he was saluted.

There was a perk though. When Calemmo related the tale (embellished as only Calemmo could) to the laughing ship's doctor in Argentia eight hours later, he was served up a salami sandwich, a huge slice of apple pie, and a generous mug of brandy.

▼▲▼

At the hollow, more St. Lawrence men with horses and oxen had arrived and were loading the last of the survivors. Each sleigh was jammed so tight that Grindley wondered if the hardy ponies could negotiate the steep hills and gorges.

Newfoundlanders, laying out the bodies of deceased sailors beneath the brow of Lawn Head, paused respectfully on Turney's approach and assured him that their remains would be transferred shortly to Navy ships docked in the harbour. Satisfied, Turney and his executive officer, Lieutenant Commander Gabrielson, bowed their heads in brief prayer before climbing on a sleigh for the interminably long and rough journey to Iron Springs.

Grindley took one look at the crowded contraptions and decided he would walk alongside the sleigh. Though weary, he felt he was in reasonably good shape. One of the new recruits hung back to walk with him. Grindley and the young recruit were the last to leave the hollow. Grindley glanced around at the telling signs that something terrible had happened here: the blackened fire remains, the dirty, beaten-down snow, filthy rags, blood-stained blankets, empty needle casings, half-burnt life jackets, empty cans of medicinal alcohol, Nicosia's whiskey bottles. His spirit recoiled at the horror of it all.

Off to the side, a row of bodies.

Grindley looked for something to cover them, blanching at the thought of having to resort to using the grimy blankets scattered about. But stronger than his aversion was the feeling that he needed to protect them. So young, and only 24 hours ago, so full of life. A heaviness settled on him. He held a fist to his mouth to stifle a sob.

Determined to have one last look at his ship, he and the young sailor made their way to the clifftop. Noting the dark clouds, Grindley told him that they wouldn't linger.

"Looks like a Blue Norther is blowing in."

The young fellow looked up at him. "Sir?"

"A fast-moving cold front. With black clouds like we're seeing now, strong northerly winds, and a sharp drop in temperature." Grindley looked at the sailor. "We've had enough of that, don't you think?"

The sailor agreed.

Below, the *Pollux* was still upright; in the flotsam, scattered bodies still visible. What a shame. They could all have survived. If they had stayed with her. Again, Grindley cursed the Navy with its almighty orders. And not a grain of sense.

Fed up, he tramped over the hills, the recruit in tow. All around them the desolation of treeless barrens stretched on and on, giving free rein to the raucous winds shrieking across it. Life here was hard fought and hard won. An hour in, they passed by Chambers Cove, unknowingly passing by the remains of the *Truxtun* hidden under Pinnacle Head. The young sailor was overcome by exhaustion. Grindley helped him down the ravine to an old shack and promised to send help. He stopped briefly at Iron Springs and reported where he'd left the young sailor. Once a man set off on his rescue, Grindley tramped the remaining 3 miles to St. Lawrence. Then through town.

Down his last hill. And aboard the USS *Badger*, docked in St. Lawrence harbour.

▼▲▼

The USS *Truxtun*: 46 survivors. 110 seamen lost.
The USS *Pollux*: 140 survivors. 93 seamen lost.

One hundred and eighty-six survivors boarded the *Brant* in St. Lawrence harbour. Some victims of the shipwrecks were recovered at sea; others washed up in coves, on shingles, and along shorelines days, weeks, and months after the wrecks.[104] Ninety were temporarily buried in the cemetery in St. Lawrence,[105] 53 in Argentia. There were multiple temporary interment sites throughout Placentia Bay: Harbour Buffet, Iona Island, Red Island, Long Harbour, Lamaline, Tacks Beach, Mary's Harbour, and St. Pierre et Miquelon. More than 60 bodies were never recovered.[106]

---

104   Rowsell, *Waves of Courage*, 160.
105   Brown, *Standing into Danger*, 347.
106   MacIntyre, *The Wake*, 200.

AFTERWORD

Eleven years after the tragic events of February 1942, the United States Memorial Hospital was built in St. Lawrence by the US government, the result of a campaign by surviving American sailors who secured the $400,000 funding to commemorate the tragedy and to thank the rescuers. The 19th and final hospital to be administered under the Newfoundland cottage hospital system, it opened in the last quarter of 1953 and consisted of two five-bed wards, two private rooms, an operating room, nurse's quarters, and records and administration.[107]

Ena Farrell Edwards, who collected food for the survivors, trekked over the barrens to Chambers Cove and Lawn Head with her box camera to take the only pictures recorded of the tragic historical event. Later, Ena refused to give up her film to the US Navy, not even at the authoritative request of Vice Admiral Bristol, US Naval Base, Argentia. A week later, she released the film to the Associated Press. Her pictures were published by *The Montreal Standard*, *The Evening Telegram* (St. John's, NL), and *The New York Times*. Over the years, Ena spearheaded the organization of many reunions.[108]

Machinist's Mate 1st Class Merlin Fred LeRouge, USS *Truxtun*, lost his life. His body was never recovered. His daughter, Dr. Nancy Yarbrough of New Orleans, and her family visited the site of the shipwreck at Chambers Cove. Dr. Yarbrough had used the benefits bequeathed to her through her father's service to attend medical

---

107   Keith Collier, "Cottage Hospitals and Health Care in Newfoundland," 2011, https://www.heritage.nf.ca/articles/society/cottage-hospitals.php.
108   Summary details of reunions are from Rowsell, *Waves of Courage*.

school. In St. Lawrence, she was invited to tour the U.S. Memorial Health Centre, expressing a keen interest in its operation and the history of the gift hospital that predated it.[109]

Felix Ed Borus, USS *Truxtun*, lost his life. His children, Judy and Robert, knew little of the circumstances surrounding their father's death. While in a dental waiting room in West Virginia, Judy learned of the disaster while reading a *Reader's Digest* article on the shipwreck of the USS *Truxtun* and the USS *Pollux*. She and Robert made arrangements to visit St. Lawrence.

Seaman 2nd Class Kenneth Landry, USS *Truxtun*, was interred at Mary's Harbour, Placentia Bay, identified by effects found on his body (a photo of his brother attending a seminary for priesthood). In August 2017, his cousin, Kenneth Privat, honoured a promise to his aunt years earlier to visit St. Lawrence and the wreck site of her son.

Charles Carman Crisafulli, USS *Truxtun*, lost his life while attempting to rescue shipmates washed overboard, as did Ensign Howard Taylor, Bill Kremple, and others. Crisafulli's brother, Fred, visited St. Lawrence during the 1992 commemorative events.[110] He too had learned details of the shipwrecks from an article Henry Strauss published in *Reader's Digest*.

Paul Daniel Pharmer, USS *Truxtun*, lost his life. In 1992, his 82-year-old widow visited St. Lawrence with her two sons. She too had learned of the commemorative services upon reading Strauss's article in *Reader's Digest*.

Stanley Irvin Rooker, USS *Truxtun*, lost his life. His niece, Kathy Rooker, attended a presentation in Virginia given by *Truxtun* survivor Lanier Phillips in which he related the tale of the World War II shipwrecks of the *Truxtun*, *Pollux*, and *Wilkes*. Kathy's father, Glenn Rooker, often spoke of his older brother, Stanley. It was his hope to

---

109   Rowsell, *Waves of Courage*, 158.
110   Over the years, starting in 1987, the town of St. Lawrence, every five years, commemorated the tragedy by inviting survivors and their families to come together with rescuers and their families as well as the community at large. These involved memorial church services, visits to Chambers Cove and Lawn Head, and a town banquet honouring survivors and rescuers.

one day visit the site where his brother had lost his life. Having spoken with Phillips, Kathy and her brother, Stanley, decided to visit the site of the shipwreck with their father. At Chambers Cove, Glenn passed his cowboy hat to his son. His brother had been a champion cowboy who loved ranching. Stanley, accompanied by Ena's son, Rick Edwards, climbed down to the beach where they placed the cowboy hat on the rocks and a wreath in the waters.

Signalman Clifford (Bo) Parkerson, USS *Truxtun*, lost his life. Parkerson, acting as the only connection between the *Truxtun* and the men ashore, stood on a rock for hours relaying messages. Phil and Nick Parkerson were present for the 70th anniversary commemorative events in 2012 to honour the memory of their uncle and great-uncle, respectively.

Water Tender Joseph Neville, USS *Pollux*, lost his life. His body was recovered by a fisherman on the east side of Placentia Bay about a week after the shipwreck. It was temporarily interred at Hillside Cemetery, McAndrews Military Base in Argentia, before being repatriated to Arlington National Cemetery, Arlington, Virginia. In 2003, his son, Joseph Neville Jr., who was only five years old when his father died, visited Hillside Cemetery in Argentia and then went on to St. Lawrence, where a tour guide took him to Lawn Head.

Machinist's Mate 1st Class Daniel Perique Gomez, USS *Pollux*, lost his life. A passenger aboard the *Pollux*, Gomez had just finished boot camp. Weeks after the shipwreck, his body, identified by his bracelet, washed ashore at High Beach, Lamaline, and was found by Cyrus Hillier while bird hunting along the coast. Gomez was temporarily buried in the Anglican Cemetery, Lamaline. His sister, Mariam Gomez Barbrie, visited St. Lawrence and Lamaline in 1990 and 1992.

Machinist's Mate 2nd Class William Kavanaugh, of Alta Loma, California, USS *Pollux*, lost his life. He was a passenger aboard the *Pollux*. His grandson, Lawrence Kavanaugh, visited St. Lawrence during the 50th anniversary commemorative events of 1992.

Gunner's Mate 2nd Class William Gustafson, USS *Truxtun*, survivor. He died forty-five years to the day after the shipwreck. His sister, Viola, and her husband visited St. Lawrence during the 1992, 50th commemorative events.

Ensign James Seamans, USS *Truxtun*, survivor. Mrs. Lil Loder, seven months pregnant at the time of the incident, who cared for Seamans at the mine house, took him home and nursed him throughout the night. He was brought to the dock on a stretcher holding Mrs. Lil's hand. He returned in 1964 with his family to see Mrs. Lil and visit the place where the wreck had happened.

Fireman 2nd Class Edward McInerney, USS *Truxtun*, survivor. McInerney, the second last man aboard the *Truxtun*, was washed into the dory Adam Mullins and his crew had launched into the seas. McInerney was taken to the home of Theresa and Robert Turpin, who spent the night by his side nursing him through the pain of frozen limbs coming back to life.[111] He and his sons returned to St. Lawrence in 1988 and again in 1992 for the 50th anniversary memorial services.

Ensign Frederick Ardel Loughridge, USS *Truxtun*, survivor. He was in charge of the rescue operation of the men on the beach. He was cleaned up at Iron Springs mine house and brought to the home of Albert Grimes for the night. He returned to St. Lawrence in 1992 for the 50th anniversary commemorative events.

Mess Attendant 3rd Class Lanier W. Phillips, USS *Truxtun*, survivor. Phillips was taken home by Mrs. Violet Pike, who had cared for him at the mine house. He made several trips back to St. Lawrence and nurtured a strong relationship with the community throughout his life. He credits the care he received that day with altering the course of his life. On his return to the Navy, he petitioned to be admitted to sonar school. He became the first black sonar technician in the US

---

111   MacIntyre, *The Wave*, 198.

Navy and went on to a career in oceanography. A civil rights activist, he received the US Navy Lone Sailor Award awarded to Navy veterans having distinguished civilian careers.

Seaman 2nd Class Edward T. Lewis, USS *Truxtun*, survivor. Lewis was hauled aboard a raft. In 2006, he returned to St. Lawrence and the home of Sue Farrell, who had cared for him. When he walked into her house, he said, "It's me, your survivor," then broke down and cried in her arms. Rescuer Levi Pike, who was 18 at the time of the tragedy, went down the cliff at Chambers Cove and returned with a few beach rocks for the Lewis family to take home with them.

Apprentice Seaman Edward Albert Perry, US Navy Reserve, USS *Truxtun*, survivor. He stayed only one night in the home of Abe Pike, who brought the young man up the cliff on his back and then carried him from the truck to his house on his back as well. Nevertheless, a bond was formed. Two years later, the Pikes named their son Eddie, after the sailor they rescued. In 1988, when he returned to St. Lawrence for a reunion, the two Eddies met for the first time.

Apprentice Seaman Edward Bergeron, USS *Truxtun*, survivor. He scaled the cliff at Chambers Cove and brought help. He returned to St. Lawrence during commemorative celebrations in 1988 and again in 1992.

Storekeeper 3rd Class Fred C. Brehm, USS *Pollux*, survivor. He jumped into the sea when Turney gave permission to attempt to swim ashore. After a night on the clifftop, he was loaded onto a dog sled and taken to the home of Julia Skinner. She gave him a huge mug of tea, swabbed his eyes with a boric acid solution, and dressed him in a large pair of wool fishermen's trousers. In a first-hand account of his experience, adapted from his personal papers by his family and published in *Downhome* magazine in 2017,[112] Brehm states that

---

112   Frederick C. Brehm, "The Sinking of the Pollux: A Survivor's Account," *Downhome*, https://downhomelife.com/article. php?id=1827.

he regretted that he had never written to her to express his deep appreciation for her help and tenderness.

Ensign Alfred Pollack, USS *Pollux*, survivor. Shortly after arriving in the hollow, Pollack, Lieutenant Bollinger, and a few others struck out on their own and followed the coastline to Iron Springs. Toward dawn, they saw the lights of Iron Springs. They were given coffee and dry clothes and loaded into a truck to be taken to various homes in St. Lawrence. Pollack was taken to the home of Albert Grimes. He returned to St. Lawrence in 1988 and again in 1992 for the 50th anniversary commemorative events.

Machinist's Mate 1st Class Walter Charles Bulanowski, USS *Pollux*, survivor. Bulanowski was on duty in the engine room when the *Pollux* hit. For many years, he resisted talking about the traumatic events surrounding the shipwreck. Eventually, Bulanowski agreed to an interview with St. John's reporter Cassie Brown, who wanted to honour the men of the *Truxtun* and the *Pollux* in her book *Standing into Danger*. In 1988 and 1992, Bulanowski attended commemorative events in St. Lawrence. Years later, his son Gerard, and Gerard's wife, Judi, also travelled to St. Lawrence to view the site.

Boatswain's Mate 2nd Class Joseph J. Janocha, USS *Pollux*, survivor. He was part of the crew who made the breeches buoy to ferry the men ashore. His son, Reverend Carl Janocha, visited St. Lawrence, toured the shipwreck sites by land and sea, and officiated Mass in both St. Lawrence and Lawn.

Signalman 2nd Class Warren (Wags) Greenfield, Seaman 1st Class Hubert Joseph Greene, and Seaman 2nd Class William Heldt, USS *Pollux*, survivors. Heldt returned to St. Lawrence in 1988 and 1992 and stayed at the Farrell's home. Greene, and his wife, Hollie, visited St. Lawrence and Lawn on the 60th anniversary of the shipwreck in the summer of 2002. Greenfield and Lawrence Calemmo also returned to St. Lawrence and shared their account of the shipwreck to a packed hall.

Junior Fire Control Technician 2nd Class Michael Hentosh, USS *Pollux*, survivor. He passed away in 1987. On retirement from the Navy, he moved his family to Florida, maintaining that he never wanted to be cold again. In 1992, Hentosh's wife and daughter made the trip to St. Lawrence for the 50th anniversary commemorative events. Seventeen years later, in 2009, his daughter, Jennifer, and her husband, Jeff, made the trip to Lawn Head.

Quartermaster 3rd Class Henry (Hank) Strauss, USS *Pollux*, survivor. Strauss had been taken into the home of Wallace Rose. He came to the first reunion in 1988. His daughter, Terry Strauss, a filmmaker from California, made a documentary about her father's experience. Completed 30 years later in 2018, "As If They Were Angels" was entered in the Mill Valley Film Festival in California and, due to the demand, was granted three showings—more than any other film entered.

June, 2007, the memory of Commodore Thomas Truxtun, one of the US Navy's first captains, was honoured in Pascagoula, Mississippi, with the christening of the fourth USS *Truxtun*. Mayor Wayde Rowsell of St. Lawrence attended as a special guest. Prior to the event, Rowsell was asked by the family of miner and rescuer Gregory Handrigan if the US Navy would be interested in a blanket their father had retrieved from the beach at Chambers Cove. Rowsell presented the blanket to Commander Timothy Webber at an official dinner before the christening ceremony. Subsequently, the Navy blanket from the shipwrecked USS *Truxtun* was framed and mounted on the mess deck of the crew bulkhead of the fourth *Truxtun*, above the honorary Missing in Action table.

Also attending the christening ceremony for the new *Truxtun* in 2007 was St. Lawrence native and naval architect Tanya Drake. In 2007, she worked in engineering and ship design in Pascagoula, Mississippi, where she learned that a new ship under construction across the harbour was to be named the *Truxtun*. While her colleagues were unaware of the historical connection between her hometown and the *Truxtun* lineage of ships, Drake, a sea cadet while growing up in St. Lawrence, had participated every February 18 in the town commemorative service memorializing the crew of the USS *Truxtun* and the USS *Pollux*.[113] Her grandparents Florence and James Fowler had taken *Pollux* survivors Walter C. Phillips from Chicago and Bernard B. Bomar from Tennessee into their home. At the christening ceremony, Mayor Rowsell was seated on the platform with the official party; Drake sat in the front row with USS *Truxtun* survivors Dr. Lanier Phillips and Edward Lewis.

The memory of the shipwrecks lives on:
In the cross that stands on Pinnacle Head,
looking out over Chambers Cove.
In the sculpture Echoes of Valour erected
in front of the town hall.
In the hiking trail commemorating the route
the eight rescuers took from Lawn to Lawn Point.
In the story board erected in Webbers at the site from
which the *Pollux* shipwreck was first spotted.
And forever in the hearts and minds of the people
of St. Lawrence and Lawn.

---

113   Rowsell, *Waves of Courage*, 179.

AUTHOR'S NOTE

As a child, I had heard tales of the *Truxtun* and *Pollux* running aground in Chambers Cove. My cousins and I spent many summer afternoons on the barrens above the cliffs. We played in the brook while the adults filled flour sacks with cranberries and partridgeberries, enough to last the winter. When the berry picking was done, they made a fire in the gully for a mug-up: raisin buns, bread and molasses, and sugary tea. In the fall, the men roamed the coastline gunning for ducks, but everyone stayed clear of the area in the winter. It wasn't until I was a teenager and Joe Doyle shinnied down the cliff one summer day and scrambled back up with a button in his hand that I began to wonder about the why and how of the disaster.

Hard Aground evolved over a period of 20 years, first in my head and then in my heart. I originally intended to write a non-fiction book. However, what moved me most was the heart of the story— the compassion, the humanity, and the heroics of those who lost their lives, those who survived, and those who rescued them. In the end, I decided to write an amalgam of both: part non-fiction, using documented information about the places, dates, events, and people, and part historical fiction, creatively telling the story using crew from the *Truxtun* and *Pollux* and rescuers from St. Lawrence and Lawn.

The St. Lawrence chapters focus on the characters of Ena Farrell, Gus Etchegary, and Clara Tarrant, all local people involved in the rescue, though the dialogue and thoughts are entirely mine. Twenty-two-year-old Ena, who captured snapshots of the tragedy, informs the role of the community rescue efforts; 19-year-old Gus was on the beach amid the rescue operation; and Clara, a wife and mother, cared for survivors brought to the mine house and later to her home.

The *Truxtun* chapters are told through the characters of Ensign Loughridge, the junior officer who took a boat ashore and was in charge of the seamen on the beach; Lanier Phillips, a mess attendant, the only Black man aboard the *Truxtun* to survive; and seaman Edward Bergeron, who scaled the cliff to bring help to his mates.

The *Pollux* chapters unfold through the characters of the ship's navigator, Lieutenant Grindley; Lawrence Calemmo, whose crew took a motor launch ashore and were stranded with a group of sailors in a cove; Ernest Califano, largely the voice of undocumented sailors who swam to shore and were brought up the cliff by the Lawn men; and the Lawn men, who have their own voice in this story.

Ena Farrell Edwards was the town librarian and my Ranger captain when I was growing up in St. Lawrence; she published two books of local history. She made it her mission to keep the memory alive and nurture connections between the American sailors and their families with the people of St. Lawrence. When I told Ena that I was writing a book about the shipwrecks, she sent me a package of her personal papers, for which I remain deeply grateful. I would also like to thank her son, Rick, who made his mother's photographs available for the book, and Cynthia Farrell, who scanned the pictures and sent them to my publisher.

There are many others to whom thanks are due: to my Round Robin writing group in Saskatchewan, who critiqued the earliest drafts before the format had gelled in my mind, and to Paula Jane, who "saw something in it"; to the archives at Memorial University for access to the Cassie Brown collection one summer while home on holiday from teaching and to the Rooms who emailed me a copy of Joe Manning's letter to his friend Gerard Ryan in Corbin, Burin Peninsula.

I would like to thank Jill Swenson, of Swenson Book Development Company, who worked with me in developing the manuscript and became my agent. From the start, Jill took a keen interest in the story and was instrumental in getting it published. I would also like to thank my editors at Boulder Books—Mallory Burnside-Holmes, Stephanie Porter, and Iona Bulgin—for their insights and expertise.

I would like to thank "my intriguing sources" (as my friends call them!)—relatives, neighbours, and friends who answered picky questions such as the correct spelling of Breakheart Hill and whether St. Lawrence was connected to surrounding communities by road in 1942. My cousins, Lon, Nash, Patsy, and her husband, Stu, answered questions about the workings of Iron Springs mine. My neighbour, Sam Tobin, promptly replied to my Facebook messages, directing me to people I could contact and providing information about such topics as gunning for seabirds! And my friend, Kathi Kelly, planted the seed to have maps included. My deepest thanks to you all.

My thanks, too, go to Wayde Rowsell. His book *Waves of Courage: A True Story of Valor, Compassion and Sacrifice* chronicles the reunions between survivors and their rescuers over the years and was my source for the Afterword of *Hard Aground*.

I regret that, in earlier years, I didn't ask my mother more about the tragedy or talk to her cousins Mick and Pius Turpin, and to my neighbour, Mr. Greg Handrigan, who were in the thick of the rescue efforts. I am grateful, though, that I was able to have telephone chats with Gus Etchegary and with Clara Tarrant's daughter, Carmel (Turpin), who passed recently.

ABOUT THE AUTHOR

Bett Fitzpatrick grew up in Newfoundland when there wasn't a child who didn't know the story and the people who carried up the cliffs the 186 U.S. service men who survived the shipwrecks of the USS *Truxtun* and USS *Pollux*. Award-winning author of *Melanie Bluelake's Dream* (1995), *Bay Girl* (1998), and *Whose Side Are You On* (2001), Fitzpatrick retired from teaching and lives in Kitchener, Ontario, where she practices yoga, hikes weekly, and writes almost every day.